The False Gospel of Guilt and Shame

Marcus J. Carlson

Copyright © 2018 Marcus J. Carlson
All rights reserved. No part of this book may be reproduced in any form without written permission from the author.
Cover Photo ©iStockphoto.com/SIphotography

Contact Rev. Dr. Marcus J. Carlson:
marcus@revdrorange.com
www.revdrorange.com

ISBN: 1984036513
ISBN-13: 978-1984036513

DEDICATION

Without a doubt, I would not be here today if it were not for the many family members, friends, colleagues and mentors who poured into my life in one way or another. I am thankful for each and every person of you. Most of you do not realize the impact you have had on my life and as a result, on the writing of this book. A special thank you to my family, my greatest support in life and first editor Jessica, and my children Micah and Abby. Thank you for supporting me, believing in me and giving me the space to serve in the ways I feel led to serve. My prayer for you all is that you will always be free from the prison of guilt and shame. Above all I owe everything to my Lord and Savior Jesus Christ who not only adopted this passionate ragamuffin, but helped him see the toxic nature of guilt and shame.

PREFACE

This book is a result of years of seeing, feeling and experiencing the tremendous power of guilt and shame. As a pastor, I have encountered countless people struggling deeply with guilt and shame. In fact, more than half of the issues I have addressed with individuals in a counseling setting have had guilt and/or shame as key issues, with most people not realizing they were even issues at all. I have also found myself working with counselors and other pastors as they struggle with guilt and shame. Guilt and shame are two of the most pervasive underlying issues affecting the health of people today.

I have written this book for one reason: to help others. I am not the world's best writer, nor am I an expert on psychology. I am not the world's best biblical scholar nor, have I perfectly conquered guilt and shame to the point where I never struggle with it. After years of dealing with guilt and shame and walking with others dealing with it, I sensed God stirring something in my heart. I began to take notes. Over a decade of notes, life, ministry and experience later, I am writing this book. I write it hoping it touches your life, convinces you of God's love for you and helps you identify and battle the lie that is the false gospel of guilt and shame. If it helps one person find freedom in Jesus and the abundant life that comes from rejecting the narrative of guilt and shame, it will be more than worth it.

Rev. Dr. Marcus J. Carlson

CONTENTS

	Introduction	1
1	The Problem of Guilt and Shame	5
2	Understanding Guilt	17
3	Understanding Shame	25
4	Rejecting the Lie and Embracing Truth	34
5	Character: God vs. Satan	42
6	Feeling: Remorse vs. Guilt	53
7	Response: Repentance vs. Shame	60
8	Motivator: Trust vs. Fear	69
9	Emotional Outcome: Forgiveness vs. Pain	78
10	Disciple to Learn from: Peter vs. Judas	87
11	Theology: Compelled or Condemned?	99
12	Gospel: Love, Grace and Mercy vs. Nothing	106
13	Spiritual Result: Spirit Filled Life vs. Legalism or Abused Freedom	114
14	The Role of Guilt and Shame	121
15	Guilt and Shame in the Church	128
	Appendix A	135
	Bibliography	137
	About the Author	138

INTRODUCTION

Guilt and shame are more than an emotional problem or challenge; they are values that can become the most powerful force in our lives, often without us even noticing it. As with many challenges we face individually and as a culture, the greatest challenge is identifying the deeper issue. In many cases, especially among Christians, guilt and shame are often two of the deeper issues. Those who attend church regularly, profess to be Christians or subscribe to a Christian worldview seem to be especially susceptible to guilt and shame.

At some point in the history of the Christian faith and church, especially in North America, guilt and shame became an important force in our understanding and application of faith. While this was unlikely an intentional act, the power of guilt and shame in the Christian church are two of the most underestimated and missed challenges the Christian church faces today. The church, its leaders and people must name and address these challenges because they have become a powerful and toxic force. Guilt and shame are not biblical values and are inconsistent with the Christian faith and with the life, ministry and teachings of Jesus. Guilt and shame are tools used by the evil one to manipulate and demean individuals inside and outside of the Christian faith, and are tools of destruction in our churches and in the world in which we live today. Ultimately, guilt and shame are a powerful force in preventing people from having a life-giving, transforming, discipleship relationship with Jesus.

In this book, I will seek to tackle the massive challenge of guilt and shame. We will look at it from philosophical, theological and practical standpoints. The first four chapters will define, describe and frame the problems of guilt and shame. Chapters five through thirteen will look at nine different ways we can frame, compare and contrast the narrative of guilt and shame with the Gospel of Jesus. A summary chart of these contrasts can be found in Appendix A. The last three chapters will examine the role guilt and shame play in different arenas. Jesus does not want us to live a life of guilt and shame. Instead, in the midst of guilt and shame, Jesus says to us, "Peace be with you" — not just once, but over and over again, Jesus wants us to find peace in every area of our lives and wants us to be whole and healthy. Only by the power of and with the help of Jesus can the guilt and shame that rule our hearts be conquered.

I too have had my own struggles with guilt and shame. For a long period of time, I was not aware that this was a core issue or problem for me. In fact, it took me a long time to realize that guilt and shame are not normal, healthy or at all biblical. My experience in working with people confirmed I was not alone in this warped understanding of the role guilt and shame play in our lives. My own work to address these issues in my life was hard, painful and time consuming. Still to this day, guilt and shame can creep into my life if I am not careful.

It was at some point in my own battle with guilt and shame that I began to work with many others who struggled with the same issue. It was, to use Henri Nouwen's phrase, a ministry of a 'wounded healer.' In the midst of my own process and helping others with guilt and shame, I began making notes, drawing charts and noting important thoughts on the issue. It has been a decade now since I began making these notes, and this book is the culmination of those notes, my own journey, walking with others struggling with guilt and shame, and countless hours of thinking, wrestling and talking about this issue. My hope and prayer is that this book would help you to examine the role of guilt and shame in your life and to be empowered to take away any power it has over you. I also hope this book will be a tool for those who help others struggling with the damaging nature of guilt and shame in their own lives. May we be able to find the knowledge and power to tackle the power of guilt and shame in our lives, our churches and the world.

MARCUS J. CARLSON

CHAPTER 1: THE PROBLEM OF GUILT AND SHAME

The first step to solving any problem is to acknowledge and define the problem. This step is true in every academic discipline, every emotional challenge, every physical illness and every organizational challenge. The most significant problems and challenges we face almost always have a deeper issue causing the problem or challenge. Far too often, we focus on the symptoms of a problem instead of the deeper causes, whether the problem is physical, emotional, organizational or cultural. The problems of guilt and shame are always deeper issues and not merely symptoms or surface problems that can be solved quickly or easily. Like other significant issues, they require intentional effort and work to identify, combat and solve for the long-term. Guilt and shame often lie in the very recesses of our heart and being. Guilt and shame are practical, emotional, theological and spiritual problems with no quick fix providing a lasting cure. More than a coping mechanism or a philosophical approach to life, guilt and shame instead permeate our emotional and spiritual being and impact every area of our life to one degree or another.

I grew up in what one might call a normal, lower middle class American family in the northeast as the oldest of two children (my sister is four-and-a-half-years younger) with two parents who loved me deeply. We lived in a small town outside the city of Syracuse, New York. All families have their dysfunction. Some families are good at putting the 'fun' in dysfunction; others take the 'fun' out of the dysfunction. I am thankful to have grown up in a family that was not the latter. I always had everything I needed, though not the minute I needed it. I also had much of what I wanted, but not all that I wanted. In all aspects, life was pretty normal and healthy for me growing up. Both of my parents came from what we would now see as larger families, with four and six children respectively.

My father's family consisted of those who could be called rebellious. My grandmother, known as Mickey, was the epitome of a matriarch. She was and will remain the most important and powerful person in that family, where pleasing and honoring grandma remains to this day the most important of all motivations. Grandma, though an imperfect person with children known for getting themselves into trouble, had very high standards and never hesitated to let anyone know how she felt about something. She was loving and gracious, but firm and clear. Few could live up to her standard and no one could ever manage to live in a way that would not disappoint her at some point. This idealism was always a challenge, but was overshadowed by her strength, love and value of family. My father's family bloodline had a lot of Swedish and Irish in it, particularly when it came to the value of being strong-willed and direct. The greatest challenge in this side of my family came in the constant worry that one might disappoint grandma. Recently at a family wedding, more than 20 years after my grandmother's death, I still heard comments and conversations framed around the fear of disappointing grandma.

The word "disappointed" is very manipulative in nature, and it feeds directly into a narrative and feeling of guilt. The word speaks more to an evaluation of character rather than a one-time mistake. It speaks to value more than it speaks to performance. It highlights one of the great challenges with guilt and shame. Guilt and shame do not speak to our mistakes, sins or shortcomings that need to be addressed, learned from or changed. Rather, guilt and shame allow our mistakes, sins or shortcomings speak to our value as a person.

My mother's family had a different set of gifts and challenges than my father's. While the drive of my father's family had been avoiding disappointing the matriarch, in my mother's family, the drive revolved around measuring up to the impossible standards of a patriarch: nothing short of perfection. The makeup of the family was primarily German and harbored the qualities of being stubborn, strong, proud and unforgiving. There was no part-way, no grey, only black and white. In addition to needing to meet an impossible standard, there was the ever constant fear of rejection. To this day there are family members who do not speak to each other over things that are nowhere as significant as they have imagined them to be. In my mother's family, guilt and shame were openly used as motivators, evaluation tools and as a form of punishment. My grandfather died alone in an apartment of one of this daughter's home.

At the time of his death, and by his own choice, he had no relationship with his other three daughters. My grandfather probably never really processed the death of a newborn son and the deportation of his father when he was young. The truth is he never really wanted to process those things because feelings and emotions were not things that were ever valued or discussed. It was a family where one was not allowed to have problems. My grandparents expected their children and grandchildren to fail. I still have not decided if that was an instinct to protect themselves from hurt or a recognition deep down that their standard was an impossible one. Anytime someone made a mistake in that family, even for us as grandchildren, that person knew it and was made to feel guilty about it. I knew in theory that my grandparents loved me, but that was undermined by the expectation to perform and conform. Guilt and shame were part of the culture of this family, and not subtly so.

The real power guilt and shame have in our lives is they do more than hurt, distract and shape us; guilt and shame become our identity. Guilt and shame carry so much power that they define us: our value, self-worth and self-esteem. Self-esteem is ultimately our confidence in how we feel about ourselves. Our feelings have tremendous power in our lives, shaping our words, actions, attitudes and perspectives.

Sometime in the 1980s, our culture elevated self-esteem to a very high place, so much that it did more damage than good. As a self-proclaimed victim of the self-esteem movement, I bought into the notion that how I felt about myself and my circumstances was the most important thing in the world, and defined and shaped everything. How we feel is important, but it is not the most important value, nor should we ever pursue a life where we are always seeking to feel good. This is not reality, nor is it possible.

When we look at the biblical narrative, particularly the life and ministry of Jesus, we recognize that feeling good all the time is not a Christian value either. Suffering, pain and difficulty are not only a reality of a broken world, they are a reality of life and they are something that we will and must face. Pain, suffering and difficulties are not punishments. Instead they are opportunities to overcome, grow and learn in spite of our circumstances. While feeling good is something that has value, the self-esteem movement elevated feeling good to a place where it does not belong. Ironically, this plays into the problem of guilt and shame causing us to devalue ourselves greatly when we fail, do not feel positive or face suffering of any degree.

While the concept of self-esteem has been warped in our culture, it still has value. It is good and healthy to have confidence in ourselves and our feelings about ourselves. We should feel good about who we are as a person. We should have positive feelings about our gifts and our place and meaning in society. Yet guilt and shame warp our view of self and demean our gifts, place, value and meaning, as well as our view of our place and value in relationships with others.

Guilt and shame also shape our self-worth. If self-esteem is seen as our confidence in how we feel about ourselves, self-worth is how we value ourselves. Self-worth is much deeper (and more important) than self-esteem as it goes beyond our feelings to something much deeper: our value as a person. Most people I have ever had a conversation with of any depth struggle with self-worth to some degree. Over and over again I see wonderful, gifted, intelligent, kind, compassionate and incredible people struggle with self-worth. Ironically, this is more profoundly true among followers of Jesus. It is ironic, because at the core the message of Jesus is that we are all worthy, we are all valuable, we are all loved. At the center of Jesus' life and message is the concept that we are all worthy and loved without condition and regardless of our performance. This is the polar opposite message of our culture today. It is not the message passed to me through both my father's and mother's families, even though they loved their children and grandchildren and never meant any harm.

One of the most painful things I experience in working with people and helping them through crisis, loss or suffering is seeing how little self-worth they have. Into my office walk these amazing, loving, gifted, passionate people who have almost everything in the world going for them. Into my office walk people with resources, information and opportunities that make them capable of almost anything. Into my office walk people who are children of God, created in the image of a God who hung the stars, formed the seas and shaped the mountains. Into my office walk people who fail to see themselves as they really are, people who fail to see themselves as God sees them. Into my office walk hurting and broken people with low self-worth, people crippled by guilt and shame.

The false gospel of guilt and shame preaches one message: you are defined by your sin, mistakes and failures. You are and never will be anything more these things, and you will forever be defined by your performance. While guilt and shame are two different issues, they are often united. Together, they have created a narrative in our world, a false gospel. It is the narrative that is the focus of this book. In speaking about the false gospel of guilt and shame, this book examines how these two issues together create a toxic story in our lives and in the world. When we fall into the guilt and shame trap, we ultimately allow our value to be dictated by our guilt and shame. This is never intentional and becomes so much a part of who we are, we rarely notice it unless someone points it out to us. Herein lies an important point: if you struggle with guilt and shame, you cannot battle it alone. This journey is not one to take in isolation. You will need encouragers and people to challenge you and be honest with you. You will need to show some vulnerability and authenticity, and most likely will need a professional counselor of some type.

Living in guilt and shame forces us to believe our value is determined entirely by our performance, specifically our sins, mistakes, shortcomings and failures. Our value should never come from guilt and shame, our feelings, what others think of us or our performance. True value comes from our identity in Jesus alone. Our identity is not based on anything external, but rather Christ in us and our identity as children of God loved unconditionally. One of the most destructive aspects of guilt and shame is that they shape our value as human beings.

The concept of guilt and shame, while a more profound problem now than in other periods of history, is not a new challenge. In the fourth chapter of John's Gospel we read of an encounter Jesus had with a Samaritan woman at a well, one of the most profound and telling passages in all the Bible. It is rich and has layers I continue to discover. It also speaks profoundly to the power of guilt and shame, as well as the view Jesus holds of people and his perspective on guilt and shame.

It is almost noon, another hot day in the desert. Jesus stops to rest at a well. The disciples have gone into town for some supplies. Jesus, a single man, is alone at the well in this town called Samaria. The people of Samaria, the Samaritans, were not valued at all by the Jews. They were considered lower class people, so much that Jews did not associate or often even speak to them at all. The Jews, these great religious people, were just too good for everyday common Samaritans. A Samaritan woman came to get water from the well while Jesus was there. This was very strange, because in most cases the women would come gather water in the morning or in the evening. They did so to start or end the day with the right supply, but also because it was much cooler then, making it easier to travel, easier to carry a jar full of water than in the hot noonday sun.

Jesus initiates a conversation with this woman by asking her for a drink. This seems innocent enough. Maybe Jesus does not have a way to get the water out of the well, except for the fact that he is able to walk on water, calm a storm, turn water into wine and fill a boat with fish. It turns out that Jesus opens himself to this woman in the most profound and humble of ways by asking her for help. This Samaritan woman, taken aback by the request, points out that he should not be asking her for this drink. He is a Jew; she is a Samaritan. More significantly, he is a Jewish man and she is a Samaritan woman. This very conversation is more than borderline scandalous in that culture. The exchange that then occurs in John 4:10-15 sets the tone for exactly what Jesus wants to offer this woman, for what Jesus wants to offer every human being. Jesus is offering more than water, more than a person to worship, more than eternal life. Jesus is offering a life that fulfills them in a way no amount of food or water ever could, an abundant life filled with meaning that could never be achieved by any accomplishments or accolades. He is offering a life filled with great value and worth that can never be diminished by culture, by the opinions of others and most importantly, by guilt and shame.

Beginning with John 4:16, we see guilt and shame enter into this conversation. Jesus asks this woman who came alone to the well in the middle of the day to go and get her husband. For our culture, this sounds like an odd request, but for this culture, it may not have seemed as odd for a man to insist on the presence of a husband as a part of an interaction with a woman. To this request, this previously verbose woman offers only a four word reply, "I have no husband."

Jesus' response is factual, telling and profound. "Jesus said to her, "You are right when you say you have no husband. The fact is, you have had five husbands, and the man you now have is not your husband. What you have just said is quite true."[1]

Imagine the expression on the face of this woman. An innocent and awkward conversation transitions to an entirely different place. One of the most interesting things about this passage is that Jesus' words to this woman about her five husbands and one live-in boyfriend carries with it not an ounce of judgment or condemnation. Jesus simply states the facts and validates that this woman, though seeking to avoid talking about her past and present with men, has been truthful. He does not talk about her failures as a wife, nor does he place blame or even indicate that her behavior is sinful. He simply notes that he knows her story and by both inviting her into this conversation and continuing it, Jesus is demonstrating that the shortcomings of this woman have no impact on his desire to offer her a life of value, worth and abundance. Her indiscretions and failures do not become a point of judgment, but rather a point of continued invitation.

The dialogue that follows, and the completion of this story seemingly focus on worship and Jesus' role as the Messiah (John 4:19-30). Jesus speaks about this woman's value as a sinner, failed wife, Samaritan and woman shacking up with someone who is not her husband. You see, this woman goes to the well a noon to avoid people, to

---

[1] John 4:17-18 *NIV*

avoid judgment. She likely goes at noon to avoid the other women of the village who know her history. She is a woman trapped in guilt and shame. Her failed relationships have defined her, and as a result her schedule, her relationships and her value are defined entirely by the guilt and shame that have come from those failures.

Jesus, instead of judging her, condemning her, even telling her she is a failure, invites her into a relationship with him. He offers her eternal life and living water. Jesus invites her not only into a relationship with the God of the universe, he does all of this in spite of all of the bad things she has done. Her one response is to go and tell everyone about this man, this Messiah and Savior who not only knows all, but connected with her and offered her fulfillment that would last forever in spite of her failures. Jesus offers this woman what he offers each one of us, a different narrative, a different story. Jesus offers this woman a different identity, an identity and value not based on her relational failures or her sin, but an identity and value based on her identity as a child of God. It is not her failure, sin, guilt or shame Jesus is interested in. He names them, but he quickly moves past them and looks directly into her heart. In this woman, Jesus does not see a failure; he sees a child of God who deeply desires meaning and value, a person who is thirsty for something so much more than can be found in a well, in a man or in a marriage. At a moment where this nameless Samaritan woman is living her life entirely based on guilt and shame, Jesus offers her hope and fulfillment.

When I read stories like this one, I often insert myself into the story and try to imagine what it would be like. Just another day going to the well and I encounter the Son of God, Jesus, the Messiah. I do not know him, but he knows everything about me. I do not know about you, but the idea of encountering someone that knows every sin, mistake, failure and shortcoming in my life makes me feel nauseous at best. Yet, Jesus is different. In this encounter, Jesus makes sure that we know he already knows all the darkness, failure, sin and mistakes of our life. There is no naiveté in Jesus.

Most importantly, Jesus takes it a step further and makes it clear in his dialogue, posture and presence that identity and value is not found in guilt and shame and instead offers a different, fulfilling, abundant life rooted in an identity and value found in the unconditional love of God. Jesus does not even speak to her guilt and shame directly. He dismisses it and offers her something better. In this moment, Jesus frees us from her guilt and shame. One of the deepest desires of God's heart is to free us from the prison of guilt and shame in spite of our performance and to restore our identity and value as beloved children of God with whom he could not be more pleased.

Important Things to Remember from Chapter 1:

- The problems of guilt and shame are always deeper issues. They are not merely symptoms or surface problems quickly or easily solved. Like other significant issues, they require intentional effort and work to identify, combat and solve for the long-term. Guilt and shame often lie in the very recesses of our heart and being.

- The false gospels of guilt and shame preach one message: you are defined by your sin, mistakes and failures. You are and never will be anything more these things and you will be forever defined by your performance.

- One of the deepest desires of the heart of God is to free us all from the prison of guilt and shame in spite of our performance, and to restore our identity and value as beloved children of God with whom he could not be more pleased.

- Our value should never come from guilt and shame, our feelings, what others think of us or our performance. True value comes from our identity in Jesus alone. Our identity is not based on anything external, but rather Christ in us and our identity as children of God loved unconditionally.

CHAPTER 2: UNDERSTANDING GUILT

I have been asked on many occasions to define and describe both guilt and shame and the difference between the two. The entire focus of this book is on helping people understand the nature of guilt and shame and their power. Understanding guilt and shame is the first key to combating their power in our lives. We struggle to not only understand these terms, but their impact. There are two distinct narratives in our lives, the gospel of guilt and shame and the gospel of love and grace found in Jesus.

When thinking about the word "guilt" and its meaning, we first must understand it has many definitions and to understand which of its definitions apply to the issues being examined in this book. First, guilt is both used as a noun and a verb. It is a thing and an action. The one definition of guilt that does not apply to our discussion in this book is the legal definition, where one is found guilty of committing some sort of crime.

When we look at the word guilt, there are two key uses that apply to the false gospel of guilt and shame. First, as a noun, guilt is a feeling. It is a feeling eliciting a sense of having done something wrong or failed. It is a feeling rooted in a belief that we have not fulfilled some goal, obligation or expectation. Understanding that guilt is first and foremost a feeling may be most important in understanding and distinguishing guilt and shame. While guilt is a real and natural feeling, it is not a healthy one. Additionally, it is not one that is at all biblical in nature, nor is it what God would want for us, something we will examine throughout this book.

The second use of guilt that is important to consider is the case where guilt is a verb or an action. In this understanding, guilt is defined as the idea of making someone feel guilty. This is the manipulative form of guilt. Much like the other unhealthy understanding of guilt, this definition is rooted in feeling, making someone feel a sense of guilt. The idea here is that making someone feel guilty forces them to accept the belief that they have not fulfilled some goal, obligation or expectation. This form of guilt does have a purpose: to manipulate. The verb form of guilt has at its core the intention to make someone feel guilty to not only create a bad feeling in them, but to try to get them to behave in a way that we want as a result. Maybe it means apologizing, feeling bad for an extended time, doing something to fix the situation, making up for the situation in some way or simply getting them to do something we want them to do and cannot get them to do without manipulating them by using guilt.

I watched many in my extended family use this approach to behavior modification frequently. My wife Jessica's family also used this as a frequent means of getting someone to do something. I have found that as a parent, it is very easy to be tempted to use this form of guilt to get my children to respond or behave in a certain way. At best, it is manipulative, deceitful, dishonoring and unhealthy. At worse, it is an intentional act used to damage and demean a loved child of God, a fellow human being who should be held in great value.

The New Testament was originally written in Greek and translated to English. Looking at the New Testament and the original language, there is only one word for guilt, *enochos* (pronounced: en'-okh-os). It is an adjective for being involved with a crime or being liable for something. It has nothing to do with feelings; rather it fits closely with the legal definition of guilt that we have today. There are other instances in the New Testament where the world guilt or guilty appears, however. In each instance, the word is referring to sin and the presence of sin in the world, in an individual or in a group. Jesus himself never talks about guilt directly, though in the English translation of the Bible the word guilty appears several times, again referring to sin.

Sin is also a misused and misunderstood word in our churches today. There are a couple important distinctions to make. First, there is the idea of sins or the things we do wrong, the mistakes we make, the ways in which we commit an offense against God or one another. A second distinction is the concept of 'capital S' Sin. Sin is the idea that by our imperfect nature we are separated from the perfect God. First, humanity tries to solve this problem in the Old Testament by the perfect obedience of the law, which as it turns out is impossible.

The problem is resolved in the New Testament in the birth, life, death and resurrection of Jesus. Jesus' perfect obedience of the law and his sacrificial death are the solutions provided by God for the problem of separation or 'capital S' Sin. What is often missed is that Jesus' death changed many important narratives in our lives. One of the narratives or stories that the death of Jesus changed is related to shame. We no longer have to carry shame because of what Jesus has done for us.

Recently, I had a friend and colleague say something in a moment of stress and frustration that was inaccurate, over the line and deeply hurtful. It was hurtful because of how it was said, who said it and what it meant to me. It was for me a trigger point, one of the small handful of things that always seems to hurt me deeply. We all have these things that bother us more greatly than others, that hurt us more deeply or cause a greater desire for justice in our hearts and minds. When my friend came to apologize to me about it, I shared my pain briefly. I knew to share it only briefly, because while he needed to know the impact of his words and would benefit from knowing more about me, focusing in on my hurt would only open the door to the unhealthy and unbiblical sense of guilt. Even in my attempt to keep it simple, my friend instantly went to the false gospel of guilt and shame. While this likely means that guilt and shame is something that he struggles with, the more pressing issue was not allowing guilt and shame to enter into this situation. My friend instantly began talking about his sin against me. I quickly retorted that the real sin was not the mistake itself, but that he would continue to live in guilt about the mistake. This is one of the most missed dangers about guilt: the moment where our legal guilt of committing and offense becomes the unhealthy, unbiblical feeling of guilt.

The Old Testament is very similar, only with more occurrences of the concept of guilt. In the Old Testament, there are several instances where we see "guilt" or "guilty" in the English translation. The primary Hebrew word for guilt, *asham* (pronounced aw-shawm'), is a noun referring to an offense. *Asham*, as is guilt, is used to talk about guilt offerings, things that one would give to God to make up for breaking the law or for being guilty of an offense against the law. Now, while we know that we no longer live under the Old Testament and live a new life under the new covenant in Jesus, we must not throw away the Old Testament as it shows us both our need for Jesus and gives us a history and a picture. It also provides great wisdom and instruction that is even applicable to our lives today. That said, the nature of the Old Testament is a culture of law and punishment, not of guilt and shame.

The real problem with guilt and the feeling it elicits is that it seeks to continue to punish a person for their shortcomings, mistakes, failures or offenses. This concept is critical to understand the false gospel, to reject its narrative and to embrace the Gospel of Jesus Christ, one of love and grace. One of the purposes of the death of Jesus is that we no longer have to continue to punish ourselves when we fail, commit an offense or sin. When we embrace guilt, we are wasting what Jesus did on the cross and spitting in the face of the love and grace expressed in his willingness to die so we might be free from guilt.

The Gospel of John, chapter 8, begins with a test for Jesus from the legalistic religious leaders. They were the "sin police" who embraced the gospel of guilt and shame. They did not like Jesus' message of love and grace and were trying to use the law of the Old Testament to trick him. They brought to him a woman who was caught committing adultery. The law stated that any woman caught in adultery must be stoned to death, and so they asked him about this law, hoping he would ignore the law so that they, the religious leaders, could condemn him as well. What Jesus does next is one of the most fascinating, beautiful and profound moments, not only in Scripture, but in all of literature and human history.

Jesus bends down and just starts writing on the ground, in the sand, maybe with his finger, maybe with something else, as they continued to press and question him, ratcheting up the pressure. Then he stood and told the mob of people yielding rocks that the one who had not committed any sins should be the first to throw a stone. Then he went back to writing in the ground. This may have been the first mic drop in all of human history. After hearing his words, the crowd began to slowly walk away, dropping their stones. It was the older members in the crowd who walked away first, for they had the wisdom to know instantly that they had failed and had plenty of sins that never earned them the punishment this woman was about to experience.

After the crowd disperses, Jesus looks at the woman gently and asks her where the crowd has gone, asks her if anyone has condemned her. Personally, I enjoy it when Jesus asks or states the obvious. It is one of his favorite tools to point out a truth without preaching at anyone, to bring us to wrestle with something important without telling us what to think. She notes that no one has condemned her to this brutal mob death that she was sure would be her demise. Then, in one of the moments where Jesus subtly, but clearly demolishes guilt, Jesus simple says, "Then neither do I condemn you."[2]

Jesus takes it a step further and gently tells this woman to walk away from the life living in sin. Most think this refers to her sins; particularly, maybe to a lifestyle of adultery. While this may be true, we do not know all the sins she has committed. I also believe Jesus is calling her to walk away from a life of capital S Sin, the living of live separated from God. Jesus does not judge, chastise, correct

---

[2] John 8:11 *NIV*

or heap guilt upon this woman; he simply calls her to a new way of living. In fact, I believe he calls her to a life that is also one that does not dwell on her sin. Living in and dwelling on our sins is the essence of life lived under the false gospels of guilt and shame and it is not the life that Jesus called this woman to, nor is it the life Jesus desires for you or I.

Guilt is a feeling, but it is not a feeling that is productive, healthy or one that comes from God, regardless of how natural or normal it might feel. Regardless of what the church preaches or the culture teaches, guilt is not of God. Guilt is something that causes us to focus on ourselves instead of God. Guilt causes us to feel the weight of our sins, shortcomings and failures instead of the freedom of the love and grace of God. Guilt makes us always feel unworthy. Guilt is focused on what we have done and distorts reality. It distorts the practical truth and the biblical truth found in the life and teachings of Jesus, the Gospel of love and grace.

Important Things to Remember from Chapter 2:

- First, as a noun, guilt is a feeling. It is a feeling that elicits a sense of failure or of having done something wrong. It is a feeling rooted in a belief that we have not fulfilled some goal, obligation or expectation.
- The real problem with guilt and the feeling it elicits is that it seeks to continue to punish a person for their shortcomings, mistakes, failures or offenses. While guilt is a real and natural feeling, it is not a healthy one.
- When we embrace guilt, we are wasting what Jesus did on the cross and spitting in the face of the love and grace expressed in his willingness to die so that we might be free from guilt.
- Guilt is something that causes us to focus on ourselves instead of on God. Guilt causes us to feel the weight of our sins, shortcomings and failures instead of the freedom of the love and grace of God.

CHAPTER 3: UNDERSTANDING SHAME

If guilt is a feeling, then shame is an identity. "Any emotion can become internalized as an identity."[3] Shame occurs when the feeling of guilt becomes internalized as such. Guilt tells us we must focus on what we have done wrong and where we have fallen short of our expectations, the expectations of others and the expectations of the culture as well as our perceived expectations from God. If guilt tells us we must focus on our sins, failures and shortcomings, shame tells us that our sins, failures and shortcomings are our identity. Guilt is about what we have done; shame speaks to who we are. The message of shame is this: our identity is found in what we get wrong, nothing more, nothing less. Shame goes beyond the making of a mistake. Shame tells us that we are a mistake, that all we do is flawed, effective or wrong.[4]

---

[3] Bradshaw John, *Healing the Shame that Binds You* (Deerfield Beach, FL: Health Communications, Inc., 2005), 21.
[4] Bradshaw John, *Healing the Shame that Binds You* (Deerfield Beach, FL: Health Communications, Inc., 2005), 21.

The definition of shame is similar to guilt in some ways. First, it has both a definition that is a noun and a definition that is a verb. Second, the definition of shame is rooted pain, control and manipulation. Shame shares the same power of guilt in our lives, though in a markedly different way. Shame and guilt allow our sins, mistakes and shortcomings to continue to punish and define us, with guilt being the continued punishment and shame allowing these things to define who we are. Guilt is about what we have done; shame is focused on who we are. Shame teaches us that who we are is defined entirely by our guilt, the feeling that comes from our sins, mistakes and shortcomings. Guilt is a building block to an identity and life of living in shame. Shame becomes our identity rather than finding our identity in Jesus, the identity we have as beloved, chosen children of God.

Shame as a noun is the hard and painful state of consciousness or being rooted in guilt and humiliation. Shame is stressful, painful and humiliating. It is living in a constant state of guilt, humiliation and worthlessness. Shame communicates we will never be worthy, and as a result our identity is found in our unworthiness. The verb shame refers to the act of shaming someone to make them feel bad or to motivate them to behave in a certain way. Much like the verb form of guilt, the verb form of shame is controlling and manipulative at worse and deceitful and devaluing at best. In this form of shame, the goal is to force someone to feel inadequate and unworthy, often in comparison to one's own standard, the standard of the culture or the perceived standard of God.

Shame as a verb is not only something we do to others, but also it is something we do to ourselves. I am one of those people who is far harder on myself than anyone else could ever be. I am truly my own worst critic. I know not everyone is like me in this way; however, I know many are. In many cases, shame comes from our own expectations of ourselves. Shame also tends to cause us to be harder on ourselves regardless of where the shame has come from. This is just another way shame can become a vicious cycle difficult to break. In so many cases, shame simply seems insurmountable. Having a high standard for oneself is a noble cause, and the Scriptures call us to continued growth, to excellence and giving our very best for God. When our failures to meet our own high standard become our focus, we have entered into an unhealthy place, a place that borders on living in shame. Shame occurs when our guilt becomes neurotic.[5]

One of the roles I have is as a professor. I have taught undergraduate and graduate students as a teaching assistant and professor at five different education institutions over a period of 17 years. It has been a great joy, an incredible experience and a humbling endeavor. Over that time, I have seen the role that guilt and shame play in the lives of students in many ways, especially around grades.

Recently, I received a lengthy email from a student about a grade she received on a small written assignment. In that email, she stated that she needed to know what she could do better, because her grade at 96% was unacceptable for her. In that moment, I had many reactions to this email, some personal, some as a pastor, some as an educator. What struck me most about her email and subsequent dialogue was that anything short of perfection was never going to be good enough for her, that the only way to really succeed or measure up would be to achieve 100%.

---

[5] Bradshaw John, *Healing the Shame that Binds You* (Deerfield Beach, FL.: Health Communications, Inc., 2005), 21.

While I love to do my best and take excellence seriously, I have learned the hard way that creating expectations of perfection for oneself is incredibly dangerous. There is no way to completely succeed, and therefore, failure is guaranteed. The pressure and stress to perform leads to a life of perfectionism guaranteeing hurt and pain personally, interpersonally and vocationally. It is a recipe for guilt, shame and burnout at best.

Perfectionism is often the self-prescribed drug we use to try to combat guilt and shame. The great irony is that perfectionism only empowers and propagates the cycle of guilt and shame. While Christ calls us to excellence, to grow, learn and give our very best, perfection is reserved for Jesus alone until Jesus himself perfects us when we come face to face with him in eternity. Perfectionism, much like shame, steals our humanity, reducing us to an impossible standard of performance rather than focusing on our personality, gifts and character. It creates an identity rooted in external measures rather than an identity rooted in God's unconditional love and grace for us. It is a blatant rejection of what Jesus did for us in his death on the cross.

Jesus does not once speak about shame, and his actions, teachings and life contradict the concept and practice of shame at every turn. The Greek word for shame is *aischuné*, (pronounced ahee-skhoo'-nay). The Greek definition may perhaps be most profound for our understanding. One of the meanings of this word is "the confusion of who one is."[6] Even in the time of Jesus, the concept of shame was clearly a perversion of one's humanity and identity. Throughout the Old and New Testament, shame is espoused as a negative value, a

---

Strong's Exhaustive Concordance: New American Standard Bible. Updated ed. La Habra: Lockman Foundation, 1995. http://www.biblestudytools.com/concordances/strongs-exhaustive-concordance/.

punishment and source of death, something to avoid. The Psalmist frequently asks to avoid or be rescued from shame. Shame is not of God. It is unproductive, unhealthy and unbiblical. Furthermore, "the feeling of shame has the same demonic potential (as addiction) to encompass our whole personality."[7]

Shaming someone else demeans, rejects and devalues them. It denies their identity as a child of God, an imperfect person created in the image of God. Shame steals and often destroys our humanity. As one colleague noted on one of my social media posts, "shame is the thief of intimacy." Shame destroys relationships and ruins intimacy in our relationships with one another and most importantly in our relationship with God. Shaming someone else is a blatant rejection of them as a person and as a child of God. Shame propagates fear and divides communities. It is at best manipulative; it is at worse destructive and abusive. Placing shame on someone else has no long-term benefits and any short-term benefits are self-serving and sinful. Shame is the doorway to hatred and is not, nor will it ever be, a value of the Gospel of Jesus Christ. Shame must not be used at all, especially as a weapon, and a church that propagates guilt and shame not only rejects the Gospel of Jesus, it commits an egregious sin and a manipulative error that often crosses the line of heresy.

At the start of the eighth chapter of Matthew, we read a story about Jesus' encounter with a leaper. Leprosy is a disease unknown in civilized parts of the world today, but it is a destructive and demeaning disease. It impacts the nerves throughout the body among other things, and is characterized by sores, bumps, cuts and more. In the time of Jesus, leapers were put into a colony together away from

---

[7] Bradshaw John, *Healing the Shame that Binds You* (Deerfield Beach, FL: Health Communications, Inc., 2005), 21.

the general public. Rejected by the religious leaders as unclean, they were seen as disgusting for their disease and its impact. They were feared as contagious and dangerous, some of the worst and most rejected of society, with family often walking out of their lives. They had to announce their presence by shouting "unclean," and it was unlawful to touch them in any way. Many of those who had leprosy lived with it for years and would go most of their lifetime without feeling the touch of another human being. They were truly shamed by the culture, by friends, family and the church.

In this story, a leaper comes close to Jesus and begs for healing, begs to be made clean. He is humble in his request, acknowledging that Jesus can make him clean, but that it was up to Jesus. Jesus of course honors his request and makes him clean and heals him from his leprosy. It is not the only time Jesus heals someone with leprosy, but this instance was unique. By healing the man, Jesus does something unheard off in that time, something against the religious law, unnecessary and unthinkable. As a part of the healing, he reaches out and touches the leper. Jesus does not need to touch him to heal him, and by touching him, Jesus has made himself unclean by the rule of the religious law.

Additionally, Jesus has broken religious, cultural and social norms. Jesus not only heals this man physically, he brings complete healing to the life of rejection, guilt and shame the man has lived in for what might have been a lifetime. Jesus destroys his shame and with his physical gesture of intimacy, offers this man who may not have ever known what intimacy was a chance to break out of the cycle of guilt and shame. He wants him to live a life free in Christ, healed in every way, a life in the narrative of love and grace. For many, the most profound part of what Jesus did in this moment is that he healed this man. Yet in understanding the nature of guilt and shame, the power of rejection and the importance of an intimate relationship with Jesus, the most profound moment is the simple touch of Jesus.

Shame is a cycle where we allow our guilt to shape and define us, influencing every aspect of our lives. Thus, shame is at the center of almost every cycle of addiction, and in most cases, is the primary cause of addictions of almost all types. Shame destroys families, friendships, careers and communities. Shame is one of the most destructive forces in the world today, especially in the church. Shame is the world of the evil one, a tool that demeans, distracts and creates an identity in us that is a great lie. What is problematic about the false gospel of guilt and shame is that it communicates that our performance (and a perfect one at that) is what is most important. What we do trumps who we are in the narrative of guilt and shame.

What matters most is who we are. Character, not performance, is what matters most—regardless of what the church or the culture falsely teach us. The story of guilt and shame seeks to undermine this truth. I do not believe the church or the culture has set out to teach, preach and live the false gospel of guilt and shame, but without question it is something that has infected every part of our society, including our churches. In light of the life of Jesus, our churches should know better. Embracing the false gospel of guilt and shame is a complete rejection of the gospel of love and grace that Jesus demonstrated and taught. Shame is both the thief of intimacy and the thief of humanity. Shame is not of or from God; shame is the work of the evil one who seeks to steal, kill and destroy. The false gospel of guilt and shame is a perverted gospel, one that we must reject at every turn.

Important Things to Remember from Chapter 3:

- If guilt tells us we must focus on our sins, failures and shortcomings, shame tells us that our sins, failures and shortcomings are our identity. Guilt is about what we have done; shame speaks to who we are.

- Shame becomes our identity rather than finding our identity in Jesus, the identity that we have as beloved, chosen children of God. Shame is a cycle where we allow our guilt over our sins, mistakes and shortcomings to shape and define us, influencing every aspect of our lives.

- Shaming someone else demeans, rejects and devalues them. It denies their identity as a child of God, an imperfect person created in the image of God. Shame steals and often destroys our humanity.

- Shame as at the center of almost every cycle of addiction and in most cases is the sole or primary cause of addictions of almost all types. Shame destroys families, friendships, careers and communities.

- Shame is both the thief of intimacy and the thief of humanity. Shame is not of or from God. Shame is the work of the evil one who seeks to steal, kill and destroy. The false gospel of guilt and shame is a perverted gospel, one that we must reject at every turn.

CHAPTER 4: REJECTING THE LIE AND EMBRACING TRUTH

In order to solve a problem, we must first be able to name and understand it. The second step is almost always one that involves a choice. What will we do next? When it comes to the false gospel of guilt and shame, once we identify and understand the problem we must make a choice to choose a different way, a better way, the way of Jesus. We can choose the paths of love, grace and life, or the paths of guilt, shame and destruction. Before we can even battle the guilt and shame in our own lives, we must first decide to reject the lie and embrace the truth of the Gospel of Jesus, the message and life of love and grace.

Richard Rohr notes, "Only the theme of grace is prepared to move religion beyond this bad and tired novel of reward and punishment."[8] Jesus brought to this world a new story, a new way, a narrative of love and grace: a narrative rejecting guilt and shame and replacing the story of reward and punishment with grace and forgiveness.

---

[8] Rohr Richard, *Things Hidden: Scripture as Spirituality* (Cincinnati, OH: St. Anthony Messenger Press, 2007), 159.

Until we change our perspective and make a conscious and intentional choice to choose the way of Jesus and seek his help, we will never overcome the power of guilt and the destructive cycle of shame.

Grace, love and forgiveness are not generally natural and are often counterintuitive, but they are the values of the gospel. These virtues are contradictory to the message of the culture. To follow Jesus and live the gospel of love and grace Jesus brought to the world is almost always countercultural. It is much easier to embrace the false gospel of guilt and shame, and is often our default posture. An intentional decision and effort is needed to embrace the way of Jesus and reject the lies of fear, guilt and shame. Love is the opposite of fear and is its antidote. Forgiveness (of self and others) and the acceptance of God's forgiveness is the opposite, the antithesis and antidote to guilt. Grace is the opposite of shame, again its antidote and anthesis. Grace is counterintuitive, but brings life; shame leads to pain, destruction and death.

One of the unintentional ways we embrace guilt and shame is in our pursuit of justice. We as a people today love justice. We clamor for it, believing we own it and are entitled to it. Of course, we are eager to see justice dispensed to others, but never to ourselves. We embrace the false message of karma that states one get what one deserves: if one does good, good will happen to them, and if one does bad, bad will happen to them. Not only is this not true, it is heresy. We all do bad, and if life is really about karma or getting what we deserve, we are all in trouble. The message of grace is we get what we do not deserve, and we do not get the many things we do deserve.

In our pursuit of justice, we often use guilt and shame as a tool, or worse yet, a weapon. We use justice, as well as guilt and shame, to assert our power over others. The

Gospel of Jesus is about trusting the Holy Spirit enough to release control and power to Jesus. The false gospel of guilt and shame is about fear, control and perverted, self-serving justice.

In John 8:12-18, Jesus enters into a dialogue with the Pharisees that gets at this issue of justice and judgment. While we are quick to judge others, nothing hurts or frustrates us more than when someone else judges us. Earlier in this passage, Jesus chooses not to condemn this woman caught in adultery and this dialogue with the Pharisees comes right after that. These religious leaders just cannot handle the idea that God would not judge and condemn, especially someone who breaks their rules and does not meet their standards.

Paul notes in Romans, "It is God who justifies. Who then is the one who condemns? No one."[9] Justice and judgement are so much easier than forgiveness and grace, but condemnation was taken care of by Jesus on the cross. In Jesus we are not condemned; we are compelled to live differently. Because there is no condemnation in Jesus, we must reject the lie of guilt and shame and embrace the truth of the love and grace of Jesus Christ. It is essential to recognize that guilt and shame—and everything they represent and produce—is a lie. We must also recognize and embrace God's truth of love and grace, free of condemnation, which compels us to live differently. It is so much easier to pursue justice and to beat ourselves up. It is easier to pick up stones and throw them at others, or throw them at ourselves.

One of the most well-known stories in all of the Bible is the story of the prodigal son. For me, it is a story that has and continues to have power in my life. Each time I read it,

---

[9] Romans 8:34b-35a *NIV*

I catch a different nuance, a different moment, a profound truth. Each time I place myself in the story as one of the characters, I find myself resonating with each in ways I never thought possible. In the story, there are two brothers. One demands half of his inheritance now, rejects his father, walks away from his family and leaves to lead his life on his own. He goes and sows his wild oats, living a life of fun and sin, a life away from the restrictions of family, a life with more money than he could ever earn on his own. Eventually, he wastes it all and has nothing: no clothing, no food, no home, no friends, no work. He finds himself taking care of pigs, and in a moment of both wisdom and desperation sees the error of his ways. He realizes that even though he told his father he hated him, took his share of the estate and walked away from his family, going back and groveling to become one of his father's servants would be better than the life he is now living. He makes his journey home expecting a response of judgment, hurt and possibly rejection and hatred. He goes hoping that somehow he can just get a job. He goes expecting justice, punishment and condemnation. He goes in a posture of desperation, with a heart likely filled with guilt and shame. Guilt and shame for his failures. Guilt and shame for hurting and rejecting his family. Guilt and shame for his poor choices and mismanagement of resources. Guilt and shame for this life of his that is in shambles.

When he arrives home, he does get some of what he thinks he deserves, but he also finds something he never could have expected. His wise and loyal older brother gives him what he expects and what he feels he deserves. The older brother heaps judgment and condemnation on him and is angry and jealous. He is in search of fairness and justice as he feels slighted both by his brother and by the response of his father upon the return of the younger, wilder brother who could never be as good and loyal as him. The older brother offers his younger brother nothing other than guilt and shame, the gospel that he already knows well and has embraced for himself. It is a lie destroying them both from the inside out.

The father's response, however, is different. He surprises all who read the story, even the most noble, optimistic and kind parents. The father demonstrates and embraces a different narrative, a better narrative. The father has embraced the gospel of love and grace and dispenses that narrative to both of his children, much to their shock and even dismay. By embracing love and grace, the father takes a direct shot at guilt and shame and ignores fairness and justice. The father not only allows his son to come home; he also treats him as the son he has always had.

In fact, he is so pleased that his beloved and lost son returns that he throws an extravagant party, using his own money, inheritance money the older son is entitled to later in life. He is so overjoyed he can do nothing other than embrace, celebrate and love his son in spite of all that has happened. In this story, we see the very heart of God in this father for his children. In this story, we see a God who rejects guilt and shame and embraces extravagant love and grace. It is not fair or just, but it is the way to life and health. It is the way of Jesus.

Furthermore, it is the way we are called to live. It is the freedom from judgment, condemnation, guilt and shame. It is the story of the Gospel of Jesus Christ in a story that anyone can understand. It is a blatant slap in the face of the false gospel of guilt and shame, the destructive lie authored by the evil one to steal, kill and destroy. We are the prodigal son. We simply have to choose which narrative to embrace: the one engrained in us by the world around us or the one lavished on us by a father who loves us.

We are faced with two narratives for our lives and the world around us: the narrative of guilt and shame or the narrative of God's love and grace. Narratives or stories have tremendous power in our lives. We use stories to teach, to communicate, to connect and to understand. Stories shape us, stories inform us and stories empower us. There are few things more powerful to the human heart and mind than stories. We experience stories shown in movies and television, stories communicated in writing, stories shared with one another and stories lived out in our lives. Jesus primarily used stories, or parables as they are called, to teach and to communicate important truths.

We all have a story, and we all embrace a larger narrative for our life. That narrative shapes our meaning, values and purpose. That narrative becomes the lens through which we understand and live out truth. We find our identity in stories. Stories also eradicate shame, particularly the story of Jesus and God's unconditional love and grace for each one of us. The story of Jesus is the one story that speaks to every human heart and life in every culture throughout all of history. It is the story of truth. It is the story that brings life and freedom from the guilt and shame that often binds our hearts and lives. It is a story that is written for every person. It would have been written if you were the only person to ever exist on planet earth. It is the story; it is the truth. It is meant to be your story, and it is our story. The enemy comes to steal, kill and destroy, but the God of love comes to bring freedom, love and grace. Choose this day and each day which narrative is yours, the false gospel of guilt and shame or the story of Jesus.

The first step in dealing with guilt and shame is to put down the rocks, the rocks you hold to throw at others and the rocks you hold on to use on yourself. There is no need to embrace guilt and shame to continually punish yourself for your sins, mistakes and shortcomings. Jesus has handled the punishment and has freed you from a life of guilt and shame. That is God's unconditional love, God's unmerited favor (grace) and perhaps most importantly, it is the truth. Choose freedom. Choose love. Choose grace. Chose the way of Jesus.

The next nine chapters are going to examine the false gospel of guilt and shame, the narrative or story of guilt and shame. Each chapter will look at a particular value and compare and contrast the way each of the competing two gospels, narratives or stories examines or lives out that particular value. On the one side, we will look at how the false gospel of guilt and shame approaches that particular value being addressed in the chapter. On the other side, we will look at how a particular value is seen in light of the Gospel of Jesus Christ, the great story of God's unconditional love and acceptance offered to all. Again, the goal of this book is to highlight the issues with the false gospel of guilt and shame and to build a way to begin to move past this false gospel.

Important Things to Remember from Chapter 4:

- Before we can begin to battle the guilt and shame in our own lives, we must first decide to reject the lie that is the false gospel of guilt and shame and embrace the truth that is the Gospel of Jesus, the message and life of love and grace.
- It is much easier to embrace the false gospel of guilt and shame and it is often our default posture. An intentional decision and effort is needed to embrace the way of Jesus and reject the lie.
- In the story of the Prodigal Son we see a God who rejects guilt and shame and embraces extravagant love and grace. It is not fair or just, but it is the way to life and health. It is the way of Jesus.
- We are faced with two narratives for our lives and the world around us, the narrative of guilt and shame or the narrative of God's love and grace. Narratives or stories have tremendous power in our lives.
- The first step in dealing with guilt and shame is to put down the rocks, the rocks you hold to throw at others and the rocks you hold on to use on yourself. There is no need to embrace guilt and shame to continually punish yourself for your sins, mistakes and shortcomings. Jesus has handled the punishment and has freed you from a life of guilt and shame.

CHAPTER 5: CHARACTER: SATAN VS. TRIUNE GOD

In this chapter, we begin to look at the various competing elements coming from the two narratives, the false gospel of guilt and shame and the Gospel of Jesus. The first competing element to consider are the two characters for two competing stories we are led to believe. The gospel of guilt and shame is a lie and is of the evil one; the Gospel of Jesus is the truth and comes from a loving God. While many Christians do not agree on the exact nature of the evil one or the spiritual realm, both exist. While we readily recognize and understand the physical realm, the same is not true with the spiritual realm. There is and has been a battle, a spiritual battle in the spiritual realm, both in the lives of individual and in communities as well. The Triune God calls people to a relationship with Jesus, while the evil one, sometimes called the devil or Satan, seeks to draw us away from the love of God.

Most people, Christians included, are uncomfortable talking about Satan. This is a mistake, given that Satan and evil are very real. C.S. Lewis, in the *Screwtape Letters* notes,

"There are two equal and opposite errors into which our race can fall about the devils. One is to disbelieve in their existence. The other is to believe and to feel an excessive and unhealthy interest in them. They themselves are equally pleased by both errors."[10] When it comes to the evil one, we can make two great mistakes: we can underestimate him or we can overestimate him. The discomfort with talking about Satan, the devil or the evil one has led to great misunderstandings about the nature, purpose and tactics of Satan.

The purpose of Satan, or as I like to say, the evil one, is outlined in John 10:10: "The thief comes only to steal and kill and destroy; I have come that they may have life, and have it to the full." This verse not only lays out the purpose of a loving God and the purpose of the evil one, it also points us to the purpose of a loving God and the evil one. The evil one simply comes to steal, kill and destroy. This is often emotional in nature, and at the heart of the false gospel of guilt and shame is the evil one who seeks to steal life from us and to destroy us from the inside out. Make no mistake, the evil one is the author of guilt and shame, and both are his favorite tools. The purpose of a loving God is to bring us love, joy, health and life in abundance. These contrasting purposes are at the center of the battle between the Gospel of Jesus and the false gospel of guilt and shame.

The evil one appears throughout the Bible in various forms. The first appearance of the evil one is in creation in the garden with Adam and Eve. From the start, the evil one, represented by the serpent, is seeking to distract humanity from the love and purposes of God. For the evil one, it is all about power. The evil one has been battling God for power in our lives and in the world from the very

---

[10] Lewis C.S. The Screwtape Letters: Includes Screwtape Proposes a Toast (New York, NY: Scribner, 1996), ix.

start. In the garden, the evil one (the serpent) tempts Adam and Eve, offering them knowledge and power, making a promise that they can be on the same level as God. He manipulates and deceives them into believing God is simply trying to hide truth from them. Again, this is a common tactic of the evil one.

The evil one is the greatest deceiver in the history of the world, and it is through distraction, deceit and manipulation that he often operates. In fact, Bradshaw states, "The demonic potential of shame can lead to the most destructive emotional sickness of self a person can have."[11] Simply put, the evil one is a lie and communicates lies. The story or gospel of guilt and shame is a lie. The truth is found in a God who loves us, in the Gospel of Jesus. John 8:44 points out that the evil one is a liar, the author of lies with no truth to be found.

Jesus himself was tempted by the devil, a dialogue outlined in Matthew 4:1-11. The devil tempts him three times, and does so when Jesus is at his weakest. Jesus is alone in the wilderness, fasting, and most certainly tired and hungry. The evil one also likes to attack us when we are at our weakest: when we have made a mistake, or are tired, discouraged, depressed, sick or struggling in some other way. In this account in the Bible, we see the devil tempt Jesus three times. There is much commentary from scholars on this interaction we cannot examine here in this chapter, but there are a few important observations as it relates to our conversation about guilt and shame.

Much like Adam and Eve in the Garden of Eden, the evil one seeks to tempt Jesus by offering him power, knowledge and material needs. He seeks to exploit Jesus' weaknesses and tries to cast doubt in his heart about the

---

[11] Bradshaw John, *Healing the Shame that Binds You* (Deerfield Beach, FL: Health Communications, Inc., 2005), 21.

love of God the father for him. He tempts Jesus to prove himself ,to prove his power, stature and importance. The evil one often uses this tactic as a part of the false gospel of guilt and shame. He sows in our hearts and minds the idea that we must measure up and prove ourselves to God, others and to the world at large.

The problem is that we inevitably make mistakes, fail, sin and have shortcomings. We create and allow an unreasonable standard that we must measure up to but can never achieve. Phrases such as, "I am my own worst critic" and "No one is harder on me than myself" have become completely cliché and acceptable in the culture and the church. While there is some merit to these concepts and they are natural for most personalities, there is at their root a potential danger. This is often a part of the problem of perfectionism, but at the very least it communicates that our value is found only in our performance. Our performance is then what gives us worth, not our character and identity in Jesus Christ.

Jesus is also tempted by the devil in this account to value popularity, to be relevant and to be spectacular. The temptation and need to be spectacular continues to grow in our culture today, especially with children and youth. One of the more disturbing stories I heard in my time working with youth came from a parent of a high school junior. The student was touring various schools, considering where he would attend college after he graduated. He was a stellar student, an athlete with great grades and test scores. He was active in extracurricular activities at the school and in the community. He was a leader in the youth ministry at the church as well. Once, when touring at a state school, the admission counselor noted his many accomplishments and impressive qualifications as an applicant (keep in mind, this was not an Ivy League school). After offering various compliments about his accomplishments, he said, "I only see one thing missing—what nonprofit have you started?"

There is immense pressure in our world today to be absolutely spectacular, to be popular and to succeed to a level that we have never seen before. Not only does Jesus reject this temptation from the evil one, his entire life and ministry rejected the notion that one has to be spectacular. The Apostle Paul notes in his letter to the Philippians that Jesus intentionally made himself a man of no reputation. Jesus, rather than being motivated by those around him or by the lies of the evil one, stands on the truth found in God. He stands on the truth that his value, identity and worth are not found in his performance, popularity or ability to be spectacular. Rather, he finds his identity as a child of God who is loved and forgiven just as he is, the beloved son of God with whom God is well pleased. There is great value in achieving many good things and finding success, but when these become our focus we enter into the false narrative of the evil one and face the danger of embracing the destructive lie of the false gospel of guilt and shame.

The book of James reminds us that if we resist the devil he will run from us. The devil, though smart, tricky and powerful, is a coward. He cannot handle truth, and his message and tactics are lies. The tactics of the evil one are few, but powerful, relying on fear and lies. The evil one seeks to distract and divide, and his agenda is to steal, kill and destroy. The evil one seeks to steal from us the abundant life Jesus offers us, the abundant life he died for, the abundant life we all want and desire. The evil one has no power over our lives other than the power that we give him, because evil was defeated at the cross and God has already won the battle, the battle over sin, evil and our hearts. It is not a matter of power; it is a matter of outwitting the evil one, rejecting the lies and embracing the truth found in the Gospel of Jesus Christ.

Contrasting the narrative of lies authored by the evil one is the Gospel of Jesus, the gospel of unconditional love and grace. The author of the truth is the one Triune God, Father, Son and Holy Spirit. The concept of a Triune God, three in one, is very difficult for most to understand, and there is a part of it that is mysterious. They are one, yet three, so how does that work? There is no fitting analogy or explanation that can communicate this idea exactly. Regardless of how difficult it can be to understand the trinity or a Triune God, it is God who is the author of truth and the author of the Gospel of Jesus Christ, the gospel of unconditional love and grace. The best way to understand the Triune God and to understand the Gospel of unconditional love and grace is to look to Jesus.

Jesus is God in the flesh, son of the father. Jesus came to save the world from sin and death, both during our life on earth and our life in eternity. He came to save us from the false gospel of guilt and shame and save us to an abundant life lived in the unconditional love and grace of God, a life of joy instead of a life of pain. Jesus also came to show us how to live and how to love. Through his words, his actions and his life, Jesus gave us not only a picture of who God is, but a picture of who we can and should be and who we are created to be. In the book of 1 John, we are reminded that Jesus also came to destroy the work of the devil, to expose the lies of the evil one for his lies. Jesus came to bring truth to the world, to our hearts and to our lives.

We often see God as one who is distant and angry. The terrible paintings of a white, scowling God in the clouds that hang in churches do not help us. The overly serious and also far-too-white pictures of Jesus in our churches do not help much either. It has been said that God created us his image, and we have returned the favor. Hanging in my office is a different kind of picture of Jesus. Sure, his skin is perfect and his hair is flowing. He is not white, because let's be honest, how likely is it that Jesus growing up in the Middle East was a pasty-skinned white man?

What is most significant about this picture of Jesus is his expression. He is laughing and not just the chuckle kind of laugh or the awkward giggle you make at a bad joke from a friend. Instead, this painting has Jesus engaging in a full-blown belly laugh. It is the only picture of Jesus in my office, which might sound wrong for a pastor. But it is the one picture of Jesus in my office because it is the picture of Jesus that we miss or forget the most, the loving, fun, joyful God who the evil one wants to convince us does not exist. I leave it there to let people see this part of who the real God is. I leave it in there to remind people, myself included, that our God is a God of love, joy and life. I also leave it there to remind myself that I should not take myself too seriously and that God has a sense of humor in some moments where as a pastor I see no humor.

As mentioned in an earlier chapter, the Triune God is the God of love and acceptance, much like the father in the story of the prodigal son. The God of the Scriptures is a God who loves us just as we are, accepts us as we are and embraces us as we are. God has already defeated the evil one and, again, the evil one has no power over our lives other than the power given by us. I often find myself saying aloud, "Go away, Satan" (though not always that gently and sometimes a bit more colorfully). The battle is for our focus and for our heart. We get to choose which narrative we will believe. We can believe the lies of the evil one, the lie that is the false gospel of guilt and shame, or we can believe the truth. We can believe the truth that is the

Gospel of Jesus Christ, authored by a God who loves and accepts us just as we are.

God is not angry and distant. God is loving, hopeful and accepting. God desires to be close to us, but never imposes. God does not go where God is not invited, yet God is always with us, standing ready to express the love of God to our lives and give us abundant life. The God of the Bible is a God of joy, not a God who keeps attendance, has a file folder (or filing cabinet for some of us) full of our sins, mistakes and shortcomings. God sees, loves and accepts us as we are, and God also sees, loves and accepts us for all we could be. Guilt and shame are not of God and break the heart of God. When we hurt, God hurts. To sum up the Triune God of the Bible in one word, that word is *love*.

Love can be complicated and yet simply revealed in life around us. As a child I grew up with pets and have always loved animals. In fact, for a certain period in high school I wanted to be a veterinarian. That did not work out, so I became the next thing, a pastor and teacher. In reality, I could never be a vet because science is not my strong suit, and I still cry when I or someone else has to put an animal to sleep. At our house in the country, we have many animals. We have chickens in the backyard coop for eggs. We have shelter rescue cats in the barn for pest control. We have bunnies in an outdoor hutch that belong to our son. We have a couple of cats inside and have had dogs since the time we were engaged years ago. In the last two years, we said goodbye to our first two beloved dogs we have had since the time we were engaged, and that has not been easy on any of us.

After their passing, we acquired two purebred Border Collies, a new breed to us. Our Border Collies, Oreo and Reeses, are incredible dogs. They are off-the-charts intelligent (they can do over 30 tricks, including basic math) and are very loving. They also have incredible energy and suffer from separation anxiety, a common issue for Border Collies. When I arrive home from being gone, whether I have been gone minutes or weeks, the Border Collies greet me with an excitement, love and joy that is unlike anything I have ever seen. They get so happy and excited that one whimpers and the other wags her tail so hard that her whole back end flails from right to left. To them, I am the most wonderful thing in the world and can do no wrong. Sometimes, I think to myself, *I wish I could be half the person my Border Collies think I am!* My border collies love me just as I am. They see me as far better than I could ever be, and they heap love all over me even when it is the last thing I want (like jumping on me and laying across my body licking my face in the middle of the night). They always want to be near me. If I move, they look to see where I am going and often move with me. All they want is to be around me and love me. For me they are just another simple and imperfect reminder of the God of love, the God of the Bible, the God of the gospel of unconditional love and grace expressed in Jesus.

God is not distant and uninterested. God is not insensitive and uncaring, nor is God demanding or cold. God is neither condemning or manipulative. God is not mean, cruel or abusive. You see, all God desires is for us to be loved and for us to be whole. Jesus deeply desires to be in a relationship with us. He wants us to know the grace of God and that we are loved without condition. Nothing brings the Triune God greater joy than simply being with us. God wants nothing but the best for us and would never want any of his children (and we are *ALL* his children) to live in guilt and shame. The truth of God and the truth of the Gospel of Jesus Christ is that we are loved by the

Triune God, the creator of the universe, and in the image of that same God, we his children have been made. Choose truth. Reject lies. Choose the Triune God who loves you. Reject the evil one who seeks to steal, kill and destroy.

Important Things to Remember from Chapter 5:

- Most people, Christians included, are uncomfortable talking about Satan. This is a mistake, given that Satan and evil are very real. C.S. Lewis, in the *Screwtape Letters* notes, "There are two equal and opposite errors into which our race can fall about the devils. One is to disbelieve in their existence. The other is to believe, and to feel an excessive and unhealthy interest in them. They themselves are equally pleased by both errors."[12]

- The tactics of the evil one are few, but powerful. The evil one relies on fear and lies. The evil one seeks to distract and divide. The agenda of the evil one is to steal, kill and destroy.

- The evil one has no power over our lives other than the power we give him.

- God sees, loves and accepts us as we are, and God sees, loves and accepts us for all we could be. Guilt and shame are not of God and break the heart of God. When we hurt, God hurts. To sum up the Triune God of the Bible in one word, that word is *love*.

- All God desires is for us to be loved and for us to be whole. Jesus deeply desires to be in a relationship with us. He wants us to know the grace of God and to know we are loved without condition. Nothing brings the Triune God greater joy than simply being with us.

---

[12] Lewis C.S. *The Screwtape Letters*: Includes Screwtape Proposes a Toast (New York, NY: Scribner, 1996), ix.

CHAPTER 6: FEELING: REMORSE VS. GUILT

In the last chapter, we looked at the two characters that author the two competing stories. We have the author of lies, the author of the false gospel of guilt and shame, Satan, also referred to as the devil or the evil one. We have the author of the truth, the author of the Gospel of Jesus, the gospel of unconditional love and grace, the Triune God, Father, Son (Jesus) and Holy Spirit. In this chapter, we will look at the primary feelings at play with the two competing narratives. These are the two primary (but not only) feelings that come when we sin, fail or have shortcomings. The feeling at the heart of the truth, the gospel of love and grace is remorse. The feeling at the heart of the gospel of guilt and shame is guilt. Guilt and remorse are opposite values. Remorse is biblical; guilt is not. Remorse is the antidote to guilt.

As discussed earlier, guilt is a feeling. Guilt is a focus on what we have done wrong, the ways in which we have sinned, failed or have shortcomings causing failure, hurt and pain. In guilt, we are stuck in our mistakes and often continue to punish ourselves for our shortcomings or the wrong things we have said and done. Guilt focuses on justice and punishment and not in the natural, healthy way, but rather in a demeaning and destructive way. In feeling guilty, we do not trust God with justice but rather assume the responsibility for punishment and justice for ourselves. The feeling of guilt as defined in chapter two is the feeling we must define ourselves by our sins, shortcomings and mistakes. It is the notion that our performance defines us and is the only thing that counts. Furthermore, it is the negative aspects of our performance that matter most. The feeling of guilt forces us to feel the weight of our sins, mistakes and shortcomings over and over again. Guilt is unworkable, and as a lifestyle it creates a never-ending, unwinnable battle.

In many cases, this feeling of guilt causes us to assume there is no turning back, no making up for and no moving forward from our sins, mistakes and shortcomings. Guilt is punitive and abusive, and it demeans and damages. Guilt is a weapon meant only for harm, with despair at its core. Guilt, as a feeling, brings with it no positive or transformative value. We often assume that by embracing guilt we are appropriately giving ourselves what we deserve, feeling what is both natural and right. This is communicated in the faith community in an even more profound and destructive way. While it may be both natural and easy to embrace a feeling of guilt, it is neither healthy nor is it the feeling God wants us to feel and embrace in moments of sin and failure.

Most significantly, in embracing the feeling of guilt, we allow our sin to define us. Nowhere in the Gospel of Jesus are we called to allow our sin to define us. Nowhere in the Bible do we see a message that our sins should define who we are and how we feel. In fact, we see the opposite in

Jesus, not only forgiveness and freedom from our sin defining us, but also a story that over and over tells us again we are saved from our sin and the burden of guilt. Guilt is far more than feeling bad about something we have said or done. Guilt is a feeling that we will never be good enough, and we can never be seen as anything more than the sum of our mistakes. Guilt is the idea we must feel bad for our sins, mistakes and shortcomings—not only in the moment, but over and over again.

In embracing guilt, we take a baseball bat from the evil one and hit ourselves over and over again, hoping that at some point we will feel we have paid enough for our mistakes and that at some point this feeling of guilt will go away if we just punish ourselves enough. We have bought into the lie that not only is God out to punish us, but that we also have an obligation to continually punish ourselves. This is not love. This is not grace. This is not the truth. Guilt is an abusive relationship where we are both the abused and the abuser. Guilt, like all abusive relationships, is never justified, never deserved. We find our justification in Jesus and his death on the cross, not in our guilt. Guilt is lonely and happens entirely in isolation. We are never more alone than when we embrace a feeling of guilt. Guilt is part of a perverted gospel that has been accepted and taught for far too long in Christian communities around the world. Guilt rejects the unconditional love of God. Guilt embraces the disturbing myth that because grace is God's unmerited favor, we can never accept the gift of grace.

If guilt then is not of God and is the primary feeling associated with the false gospel of guilt and shame, what feeling is best associated with the Gospel of Jesus? The Gospel of Jesus does address how we should feel and react in the midst of our sins, mistakes and shortcomings. In preaching a narrative and life of forgiveness, Jesus points us to a feeling that helps us find self-forgiveness in the midst of our sins. That feeling is remorse. If guilt is the feeling that our sins define us, then remorse is the feeling that recognizes our sins, mistakes and shortcomings for what they are: sins, mistakes and shortcomings. Guilt is the feeling that we should be defined by and continually punished for our sins, mistakes and shortcomings. Remorse is the feeling of contrition, sadness or regret for something. While guilt is perpetual, remorse is temporary. Guilt does not have an ending or a solution, but remorse, however, does. Having regret (remorse) is healthy. Living in regret (guilt) is unhealthy. Remorse is the opposite of guilt, and remorse is also the antidote to guilt.

While Jesus has saved and freed us from our sins and their life-ending consequences, Jesus does call us to a healthy recognition of our sins and the role they play in our life and relationships. Remorse is the healthy recognition of our sins, and it is the recognition we have sinned and that while our sins do not define us, they do exist and they are outside of God's ideal design for our lives. We all sin and have sin in our life. It turns out that despite our efforts to control every aspect of our lives and achieve perfection, we simply are not perfect. We fail, sin and make mistakes intentionally and unintentionally. We have shortcomings. While a gift, our personalities have sharp edges that sometimes hurt others. It turns out that all of this is part of being human. If we all make mistakes, sin and have shortcomings, then what is next?

It turns out that the issue is not primarily our sins, mistakes or shortcomings, but what we do with them. This concept is at the very heart of this book and is a critical underpinning of every single chapter. There are two paths we can take when we fail, sin or make a mistake. We can take the healthy path, the path of life, the path lit by truth, or we can take the unhealthy path, the path of destruction, the path lit by lies. Guilt says, "I am wrong" and shame says, "I will never be anything more than the worst parts of me and the worst moments of my life." Remorse is saying I was wrong and I apologize.

In embracing remorse, we name our sin, shed light on the truth and find a way to move on from our sins, mistakes and shortcomings. In accepting the feeling of remorse and rejecting the feeling of guilt, we can find resolution, wholeness, hope and life. In remorse, there is both a way out and a way forward as it inspires healing by being healthy, hopeful and honest. Remorse is also loving and gracious. Remorse is the God- and people-honoring response when something is not as it should be, honoring our worth as individuals, embracing the truth and allowing forgiveness, not punishment as the priority. Actually, remorse is an essential component of forgiveness, and forgiveness is central to the Gospel of Jesus. It is the way of Jesus when we fail, make mistakes and hurt others, because it is both a teacher and a healer.

Forgiveness was never intended to limit our forgiveness of others or the forgiveness of others offered to us. While we are called to forgive others and should seek forgiveness in the midst of our sins, we also must embrace forgiveness for ourselves. It is often easier for many people to forgive someone else for something they have said or done, yet it is not so easy for many to forgive themselves. Remorse is the starting point to health, making things right and forgiving yourself and the path to embracing the unconditional love and grace of God. Remorse is the way of Jesus, the way to life.

Important Things to Remember from Chapter 6:

- In guilt, we are stuck in our mistakes and often continue to punish ourselves for our shortcomings or the things we have said and done wrong. Guilt focuses on justice and punishment—not in the natural, healthy way, but rather in the demeaning and destructive way.

- Guilt is an abusive relationship where we are the abused and the abuser. Guilt, like all abusive relationships, is never justified, never deserved. We find our justification in Jesus and his death on the cross, not in our guilt.

- In preaching a narrative and life of forgiveness, Jesus points us to a feeling that helps us find self-forgiveness in the midst of our sins. That feeling is remorse. If guilt is the feeling that our sins define us, then remorse is the feeling that recognizes our sins, mistakes and shortcomings for what they are: sins, mistakes and shortcomings.

- If we all make mistakes, sin and have shortcomings, then what next? It turns out that the issue is not primarily our sins, mistakes or shortcomings, but what we do with them. This concept is at the very heart of this book, a critical underpinning of every single chapter. There are two paths we can take when we fail, sin or make a mistake. We can take the healthy path, the path of life, the path lit by truth, or we can take the unhealthy path, the path of destruction, the path lit by lies.

- In embracing remorse, we name our sin, shed light on the truth and find a way to move on from our sins, mistakes and shortcomings. In accepting the feeling of remorse and rejecting the feeling of guilt, we can find resolution and wholeness; we can find hope and life.

CHAPTER 7: REPENTANCE VS. SHAME

Having investigated the two characters who have authored the competing narratives and having also dissected the two primary feelings at the heart of these two narratives, we come now to the primary emotional and internal response. If we embrace the story of guilt and shame, the lie that is this false gospel, we end up having an internal, emotional response of shame. If we want to embrace the truth that is the Gospel of Jesus, the story of God's unconditional love and grace offered freely to us out of love, then we must embrace a posture of repentance, not shame.

Guilt is a feeling; shame is an identity. In embracing shame and its lies, we are embracing something toxic. In embracing shame, we allow our sins, mistakes and shortcomings to define not only who we are, but our worth as human beings. Shame preaches we are and never will be anything more than the sum of our failures and mistakes. The end result of shame is always the same: self-hatred. In the book of Matthew is a powerful story that gives us a solution to this destructive cycle. In attempt to trick him, Jesus was once asked which of all the laws was greatest. The idea was that no matter what he said, he would be wrong because no law could be greater than another.

As usual, Jesus was ready and avoided the trap while turning the question and the questioners on their heads and communicating an important truth. That is the powerful thing about the life and teaching of Jesus: he turned everything upside down. Jesus in his answer said that the greatest law, the greatest of all the commands, was to "love the Lord your God with all your heart, soul, strength and mind and to love your neighbor as yourself."[13] Many people know this command, even those who are not Christians and have never attended church. What most people miss, however, is that Jesus is doing more than saying love God and love others. Hidden in the second line in the second greatest command is actually a third charge. Love yourself.

God is love. He loves you and wants you to love others. He also wants you to love yourself. Shame makes love of self impossible, and nothing could be more outside God's desires than self-hatred. Shame, like guilt, is an abusive relationship where you are both the abused and the abuser. Shame is a rejection of your identity, value and worth as a human being. It is a rejection of your identity as a beloved, chosen, child of God with whom God is well pleased. Shame is so loud in its self-hatred and self-rejection that it can drown out the message of love and acceptance God has for you. It is a rejection of God's love, grace and forgiveness, and it spits in the face of a Jesus who died on the cross out of love for you.

---

[13] Matthew 25:37-39 *NIV*

Shame leads to a toxic and destructive life of despair. There is no hope in shame: no way out, no joy, no life. Shame is a cycle and a perversion of the Gospel of Jesus Christ, the story of unconditional love and grace. Shaming is easy; forgiveness is hard, especially when it comes to forgiving ourselves. Yet Jesus is clear: we are to both love and forgive ourselves. This message is communicated in the greatest commandment, in countless stories and encounters, and directly and subtly in many teachings. From the woman caught in adultery, to the blind man and the prodigal son, over and over again Jesus communicates a message of acceptance, love and forgiveness.

I find it hard to forgive certain people and certain things, while finding it easier to forgive others. It is easier to forgive a close friend. It is easy to forgive someone who forgot about a meeting. It is harder for me to forgive someone who hurts one of my children—or any child, for that matter. It is harder for me to forgive someone who has continually been nasty and hurtful. We all have these categories and instances, but if you are anything like me, someone who has had to wrestle with guilt and shame, chances are that the hardest person to forgive is yourself. It is much more common than we realize and a much bigger piece of the guilt and shame puzzle than we are willing to admit.

Shame is a lie and not of God. Shame is unhealthy and destructive and not the path to abundant life. It tears at the very fibers of our identity and demeans the many great qualities we have been given. Shame destroys potential and is like an infection spreading throughout our bodies as it defines and takes over every aspect of our lives. You were not, are not and never will be defined by your sins, mistakes and failures. You are a child of God, not a sum of your failures and shortcomings. You would never want anyone you love to embrace shame, so it is not what you ever should want for yourself.

Shame forces you to live in self-hatred. We underestimate the power and the falsehood of self-hatred. Not only is it very powerful, but it is also wrong. In all honesty, it is an insult to the love of God expressed through Jesus' life and death. Self-hatred often seems like the easier path, but it is not the path of God, the way to abundant life. We have convinced ourselves that some amount of self-hatred is necessary, but nothing could be further from the truth. Self-hatred is not humility. You are created in the image of God and are loved, not hated.

The last part of the greatest commandment is the love of self. Yet hatred, including self-hatred, is far too common in Christian circles. We hate ourselves and others, as well as the actions and beliefs of others. We tell ourselves we must love the sinner and hate the sin, but that too is false. We are called to love everyone, including ourselves. The only thing we are ever called to hate is our own sin. Understand, however, that the hatred of one's own sin is an entirely different matter than self-hatred, a distinction often missed, yet crucial.

The opposite of shame is repentance. It is also its antidote and God's way to the path of forgiveness, health and life. The word repent means to turn or to turn around. Like most men, I really do not like ever to ask for directions. Before GPS and phones that could say where to go, I would try to figure out the way to get somewhere on my own, often learning from practice, both successful and unsuccessful. Today, when I get lost, my phone tells me and reroutes me. In the past, when I got lost, I would wander until I found my way, figured it out or gave up. My wife on the other hand likes maps, and her first response to being lost (before the phone) was to ask someone for directions.

Sometimes in life, whether through our own efforts or with the help of others, we need to turn around. Sometimes we are just going the wrong way, whether intentionally or not. When we fail, make mistakes and sin, we need not only to have remorse, we need to make it right, learn from it and change our ways. Pain, failure, mistakes and sin are great teachers, and rather than being a destructive force in our life, they can bring us health, growth and transformation. Repentance is not only chasing direction when we get it wrong, it is an opening to transformation. If I am honest, most of my greatest lessons have come through pain, failure, sin and mistakes. I would never choose to learn or grow that way; however, I have found when I embrace repentance I find greater (and quicker) healing and wholeness.

Understand, there is a difference between the sentiment that comes with the word "sorry" and the word "apologize." Sorry has become quite glib and meaningless today. It is just a way to brush something off rather than deal with it. When we are simply sorry, we often never really let go. When we apologize, we often make a more clear and distinct recognition of the situation and shortcoming and are able to move on from it. Sorry often means we feel guilt, shame and regret; apologizing means we recognize the issue and want to move forward. Repentance means we will say and do differently and better in the future. Shame says we have not only done wrong, but we are wrong, broken and cannot be fixed. Repentance says it is time to turn around and try something different. Repentance is a hope-filled adventure, while shame is a life-draining chore.

God will always love you just as you are, and he will never stop loving you. As a parent, nothing my kids say or do can ever stop me from loving them. Sure, I may not like them in a given moment; I might be angry, frustrated or sad, but I will never stop loving them. What is so amazing about the Gospel of Jesus and the unconditional love of God is that God's love for you and for me is bigger and more certain than my love for my own children could ever be. Think about it for a minute. Why would I ever want anything other than health, wholeness and the best for my children? How then could God want anything other than the very best for us, his chosen, beloved children? How could God ever want us to live in a life of shame?

My friend and colleague, Dan Bellinger, once noted that "our God wastes nothing." It is an idea I have held on to since he said it. God takes ordinary things and makes them extraordinary. He takes good things and makes them great. The God of love takes the bad things, takes our sins, mistakes and shortcomings and makes good with them—but only if we embrace repentance and reject shame. Shame brings with it continual defeat, but repentance brings us victory over all of our mistakes and failures. I am not a very competitive person, but I still do not know anyone who likes to lose and there are not many things sweeter than finding victory over your mistakes and failures.

Someone once told my wife, Jessica, and I that our marriage would never last. Challenge accepted. We have been married only for a short (or long depending on the day!)15 years. In that time, we have had great moments and ugly ones, victories and failures. We are imperfect people, spouses and parents who love their kids deeply. The marriage and parenting gig is far harder than ever advertised. Yet, in spite of all the ups and downs, we are still at it, having fun more often than not, still in love, giving our kids something better than the good thing we had and doing all we can to make a difference in the world. I get to lead a church, teach college and graduate students, write and travel to speak and teach. Jessica gets to work with struggling students, assist teachers, teach college students, impact education legislation and teach young ones how to swim. We have a great life, an abundant life in fact. The marriage that was never going to last has made us better, and we hope to continue to make a difference in the world. As a not-so-competitive person, it is a sweet victory that only gets sweeter—and it happened in the midst of and in spite of many sins, mistakes, failures and shortcomings along the way. Turns out something good came of this doomed marriage after all. God wastes nothing.

In shame, performance defines us. In repentance, possibility defines us. Yet it is a choice. At the heart of repentance is forgiveness: God's forgiveness of us, our forgiveness of others, others' forgiveness of us, and most important and profoundly, our forgiveness of ourselves. Shame leads to despair, but repentance leads to hope. Hope is a lot more fun and also more productive. Hope is the message and way of Jesus, and it is the message and way to abundant life. What is your response when you fail, sin or make mistakes? Do you feel guilt and embrace shame, or do you and will you feel remorse and embrace repentance, not only dealing with failure in a healthy way, but finding victory over it and making something good, perhaps even great, out of it? Choose life. Choose hope. Choose repentance. Choose Jesus.

Important Things to Remember from Chapter 7:

- In embracing shame, we allow our sins, mistakes and shortcomings to define not only who we are, but our worth as human beings. Shame preaches that we are and never will be anything more than the sum of our failures and mistakes. The end result of shame is always the same: self-hatred.

- Shame leads to a toxic and destructive life of despair. There is no hope in shame, no way out, no joy, no life. Shame is a cycle and a perversion of the Gospel of Jesus Christ, the story of unconditional love and grace. Shaming is easy; forgiveness is hard, especially when it comes to forgiving ourselves.

- You were not, are not and never will be defined by your sins, mistakes and failures. You are a child of God, not a sum of your failures and shortcomings. You would never want anyone you love to embrace shame. It is not what you ever should want for yourself.

- Remorse is saying, "I was wrong and I apologize." Repentance means that you say and will do differently and better in the future. Shame says, "I not only have done wrong, I am wrong, broken and cannot be fixed." Repentance says, "It is time to turn around and try something different." Repentance is a hop- filled adventure, while shame is a life-draining chore.
- In shame, your performance defines you. In repentance, possibility defines you. It is a choice. At the heart of repentance is forgiveness: God's forgiveness of you, your forgiveness of others, others' forgiveness of you, and most important and

profoundly, your forgiveness of yourself. Shame leads to despair. Repentance leads to hope.

CHAPTER 8: MOTIVATOR: TRUST VS. FEAR

Motivation is a powerful thing. It dictates our actions, priorities, preferences, performance, character, decisions and much more. When we embrace the false gospel of guilt and shame, we become motivated primarily (and sometimes entirely) by fear. To be clear, just because someone is motivated by fear does not mean that person has embraced the false gospel of guilt and shame. However, those who have embraced the lie of this false gospel are almost always motivated by fear, perceived and real. Those who embrace the Gospel of Jesus will be motivated by trust, primarily trust of God. What motivates us often controls us, especially when we are acting out of instinct or in a moment.

We rarely think about what motivates us, and this is both a great problem and a challenge. We also rarely evaluate how others are trying to motivate us. Sure, we know when someone is overtly trying to manipulate us, but we often miss it when marketers or media outlets try to use fear to motivate our viewing and shopping habits as well as our view of ourselves or the world. If we are honest, we are all motivated much more by fear than we are willing to admit. Other than moments where there is genuine physical danger, this is almost always a bad thing. In fact, we know things about how our body reacts to fear and the negative impact that can have on decision making. Brain researchers are starting to dig into how fear impacts the brain, while media, government and business are utilizing fear as their primary method of motivation and communication both as a tool for distraction and manipulation. Our inhibitions, logic, empathy and worth are compromised when we are driven by fear.

My most memorable, simple and superficial example of this was when I was working for a camp in Virginia for part of a summer. I was on the maintenance crew for this camp for teenagers. One of my more significant fears is snakes. It is a fear I inherited from my mother, both environmentally and genetically, and if you read the story of creation and the Garden of Eden, it is even a bit biblical! One of my growing moments in this fear (I am growing in this fear, but still have a distance to go) came at the camp that summer. There were lots of snakes there and snake problems. Not just garden or garter snakes, but the bad ones such as water moccasins, poisonous snakes that can travel on land or in water. There was a pond at the camp, and the maintenance crew would be called when a water moccasin would get into the pond, and the crew removed it to keep the campers safe. I always stayed in the truck, and I often did not want to be that close.

There were also rattlesnakes, and one day as I was walking on one of the camp roads after lunch I suddenly heard a noise and stopped. Yes, that noise, that rattle noise, yes, that rattlesnake noise! I froze in what was one of the scariest moments of my life. I looked down and three feet in front of me, curled up on the road, was a six-foot rattlesnake. Its tail and head were up and pointing at me. It was in aggression mode. I am pretty sure I wet my pants a little (not ashamed to admit that). My first instinct— after my mild heart attack—was to run. I could feel the fear. I was sweating and shaking. I thought my heart was going to come out of my chest. I could feel my blood pressure rising.

Now, luckily in that moment, I remembered what I had been told to do, which was not to run (right or wrong). Given that there had been some bites and attacks, the training was to not move, but to shout and waive your arms, as movement above the waist was not as big a deal. I still do not know to this day if that is true, but I went with it. I started shouting like a middle school girl at a concert, waving my arms as if my life depended on it (which, by the way, I believed to be the case). The rest of the crew saw the chubby high school graduate going bonkers and headed my way. They got the snake's attention as I backed away and then shot the snake's head off. Though this happened 20 years ago, I can still see it all unfold as if it was yesterday.

I went back to my room, changed my clothing, cried and composed myself before going back to work. I jumped at every noise as I walked for at least a week. The crew was in the kitchen, and I went to meet them. They were cooking something, which was unusual for them. I asked what it was, and they informed me it was my new friend, the rattlesnake. Now I was grossed out and traumatized. Also, I am not an adventurous eater, especially back then, and could not fathom why someone would eat a snake, let alone a poisonous one. They offered me some and you know what, I said yes anyway. It tasted like spicy chicken. I made some progress on my fear that day, but my blood pressure still goes up telling the story.

The truth is that it is easier to fear than to trust, easier to worry than to be confident. Fear is just the easier and seemingly more natural route. When you embrace the false gospel of guilt and shame, it also feels like it is the only route. The truth is that if that snake had bitten me that day, I would have probably been okay, at least physically. I probably could have run, even as a chubby kid, and it's unlikely the snake would have chased me. While I did manage to get out of the situation, my logic, perspective and beliefs in that moment were deeply flawed. It was not one of my finer moments in life.

There are few things in this world as powerful as fear. For some, fear not only motivates their words and actions; it shapes them. It defines their perspective and worldview, incapacitating them at a moment's notice. It is unpredictable, irrational and overwhelming. Fear is a barometer on the one hand and a weapon on the other, and like a prison where we feel out of control. Fear muddies the waters, causing us to be unable to see clearly. Fear's most powerful quality is that it shapes and changes our perspective.

Perspective is far more important than we realize. One of my favorite stories I ever used in a sermon came a couple years ago when we were dropping our children off for church camp. We were walking along the road at camp (don't worry, no snake story this time) for an opening presentation before we were to leave. As I came up the hill and around the corner, I saw something quite odd. Right in front of me on that beautiful, sunny day was the lake. Something was not right with it though. It was the strangest color green I had ever seen, green like the river in Chicago on St. Patrick's Day. Green like a mint milkshake or like radioactive slime. I stopped in my tracks and exclaimed my concern to my wife. At first, she ignored me, but I persisted and was not moving until I figured out what was wrong with this lake that my children would be swimming in. I told her it was the strangest color green, and she told me I was crazy. How could she not see it? As I was about to protest again, I decided to whip off my sunglasses for dramatic effect to prove my point. Then I saw it. It hit me instantly. It was not green and nothing was wrong with it. Sunglasses! You idiot, your sunglasses! The image I thought I was looking at was nothing like the reality because of my perspective. Perspective is powerful, and a perspective driven by fear is perhaps the most powerful, dangerous and toxic of all perspectives.

The word fear appears in the Bible often, depending on what translation you read and which scholar you listen to. At minimum, it appears more than two dozen times, and at maximum it is thousands. Some argue "do not fear" appears 365 times, the exact number of days in a year. In most of the encounters with God from Moses to Mary, when God appears the first words written are, *"Do not be afraid."* God does not want us to live a life of fear, especially not fearful of the God who loves us. Sure, the Bible talks about fearing the Lord, but that is more about honor, respect and awe, not being scared. God is to be loved and God loves. He does not want us to fear. Fear as a motivator is not at all biblical. Some of the most divisive historical moments came from misplaced fear, and some of the most atrocious tragedies were motivated by (usually false and misplaced) fear.

Fear as a motivator is manipulative, deceitful and destructive. At best, fear is, at least for a moment, a distraction from what matters. Distraction is a favorite technique of the evil one. Living in and being motived by fear does not give us life, it is not healthy, it will not make us whole and it rarely solves any problems, especially meaningful or complicated ones. When motivated by fear, we surrender power and control over to our circumstances or to others. In this way, the false gospel of guilt and shame gives away power over our life, our decisions, our perspective and our relationships. One of the often understated dangers of buying into the false gospel of guilt and shame and the lies of the evil one comes in this way. When fear becomes our motivator, we lose power and control over our lives. At certain points, it becomes noticeable: emotionally crippling at worst, overwhelming at best.

Fear has more than one opposite. Both love and trust are opposites to fear as well as solutions and antidotes. When examining the impact of the false gospel of guilt and shame and how it shapes our life, trust is imperative. If fear becomes the motivator under the false gospel of guilt and shame, then trust is and should be the motivator when we live in the truth of the Gospel of Jesus, the narrative of God's unconditional love and grace. Trust is hard, yet essential. Trust is scary, yet freeing. Trust brings with it great risk, but even greater reward. Those who are motivated by trust assume and find the best in others and in situations. Those motivated by trust are driven by hope, potential and possibility.

The word faith is an essential part of the Christian vocabulary, life and worldview. In many instances, when the word "faith" in the Bible is translated to the original language, it literally means "trust." Trust is an essential part of its definition. Trust is a journey, but it is our one great, brave, bold act as followers of Jesus. When we are motivated by trust, our trust rests in God and it is our trust of God motivating us rather than external circumstances or the people around us. Most of all, when we embrace the Gospel of Jesus, the story of God's unconditional love and grace, over time we grow in our trust that God really does love us, without condition, just as we are. Indeed, it is true as Manning writes:

> "The splendor of a human heart that trusts it is loved unconditionally gives God more pleasure than Westminster Cathedral, the Sistine Chapel, Beethoven's "Ninth Symphony", Van Gogh's "Sunflowers", the sight of 10,000 butterflies in flight, or the scent of a million orchids in bloom."[14]

Trust is a process and it is not in our nature and natural instinct to trust God, especially if we have or are wrestling with guilt and shame. Trust is at the heart of God's desire for us, and the heart that is motivated by trust of God is the healthiest of all. "Trust is our gift back to God, and he finds it so enchanting that Jesus died for love of it."[15]

My most meaningful and important relationships are founded on, centered in and strengthened by trust. In marriage, parenting and friendship, trust is the cornerstone of healthy relationships. As it is with human relationships, growing in our trust of God is a process that takes time, but unlike human relationships, God will never fail us. When we are motivated by trust, we are filled with hope rather than with fear. When we embrace the unconditional love and grace of God, our perspective changes and we see things differently. Trust is a prerequisite to hope, and hope makes anything possible. Where fear is filled only with negativity, control and limitations, trust is full of hope, freedom and potential. We are taught from a young age that trust is dangerous and harmful, but that is in fact a lie.

---

[14] Manning Brennan, *Ruthless Trust: The Ragamuffin's Path to God* (New York, NY: HarperCollins, 2009), 22.
[15] Manning Brennan, *Ruthless Trust: The Ragamuffin's Path to God* (New York, NY: HarperCollins, 2009), 22.

Freedom, possibility and abundant life come in being motivated by trust, not by fear. As a parent, I do not want my children to fear me, as in being afraid of me. I do want them to listen to and respect me. Above all else, I want them to know they are loved by me and they can trust me. I want them to trust I have in mind what is best for them, that I love them deeply and that I would never want any harm to come to them.

When we are motivated by a trust of God, we put power back in the right place. We take fear out of our lives. We take the power away from the people, circumstances, mistakes and failures that might harm us and put the power back in a God who loves us and will never fail us. When we trust God, we do not lose control or freedom; rather we find it and we begin to break through into the abundant life that the God who loves us without condition just as we are has in mind for us. If we have to put our trust in someone, who could be better to trust than Jesus?

Important Things to Remember from Chapter 8:

- Motivation is a powerful thing. It dictates our actions, priorities, preferences, performance, character, decisions and much more. When we embrace the false gospel of guilt and shame, we become motived primarily (and sometimes entirely) by fear.

- The truth is it is easier to fear than to trust. It is easier to worry than to be certain. Fear is just the easier and seemingly more natural route. When we embrace the false gospel of guilt and shame, it often feels as if it is the only route.

- Fear as a motivator is manipulative, deceitful and destructive. At best, fear is—at least for a moment—a distraction from what matters. Distraction is a favorite technique of the evil one. Living in and being motived by fear does not give us life, it is not healthy, it will not make us whole and it rarely solves any problems., especially meaningful or complicated ones.

- When examining the impact of the false gospel of guilt and shame and how it shapes our lives, trust is imperative. If fear becomes the motivator under the false gospel of guilt and shame, then trust is and should be the motivator when we live in the truth of the Gospel of Jesus, the narrative of God's unconditional love and grace.

- When we are motivated by a trust of God, we put power back in the right place. We take fear out of our lives. We take the power away from the people, circumstances, mistakes and failures that might harm us and put the power back in a God who loves us and will never fail us.

CHAPTER 9: EMOTIONAL OUTCOME: FORGIVENESS VS. PAIN

Most often, the greatest consequences of embracing and living in guilt and shame is the emotional damage and pain that comes with guilt and shame. As we look at the two narratives, we see two distinct emotional outcomes. Whether we embrace the false gospel of guilt and shame or choose instead to embrace the Gospel of Jesus Christ, there will be a clear emotional outcome. The truth that we choose to embrace brings with it an emotional result. This result comes in the moments in which we choose a story to embrace, over time and throughout the whole of our lifetime. The natural emotional outcome of the false gospel of guilt and shame is something important to understand, for it is something both powerful and real.

God is not disappointed in you. Stop for a moment and read that again. *God is not disappointed in you.* To be honest, I hate the word "disappointed" (along with the word "sorry"). It has value, but not in the way often used. It is great to use when reflecting on situations, things or experiences. It is terrible to use on people. For example, I can be disappointed that my football team is not playing well this year. However, to say I am disappointed in my son or daughter is an entirely different thing. When used on something other than a person, the word disappointment is clear and helpful. When used on another human being, the word is demeaning, humiliating and propagates guilt and shame. It is hard to avoid the word, especially as a parent, but in the now-rare moments it slips out, I can hear the toxic power of "I am disappointed in you" as it damages and demeans my children and sends them a message that they just are not good enough.

Now, this is not to say that I should not express my feelings about the negative, unhealthy or inappropriate actions of my children. As a parent, I have a responsibility to be honest with my children and to guide them both in the good and the bad. Instead, I have to find better, but also accurate and appropriately strong words to use with my children. "I am frustrated with this situation," "I am angry," "this is hurtful," "I am frustrated with your decisions," "I believe you made a poor choice," and many other words can help communicate important feelings and truth without demeaning someone else and encouraging the self-hatred that comes with guilt and shame.

Once, while serving as a youth pastor of a large church in Colorado Springs, I was getting ready for an event. About an hour before the event, one of my volunteers walked into the room with his son. They were coming to help with setup, dinner in hand. They were arguing with one another as they came in, which of course for a middle school boy and his parent is not an unusual thing—something my wife and I know well. The argument reached a crescendo of sorts when the son blurted out, "Dad, I hate you." In a moment that I will never forget and one that has become an important illustration for me in many situations, in a moment where I as a younger parent learned more than I could have in a three-hour class, came the father's response. "Sam, (name is changed, of course), words mean things."

Not eloquent or grammatically perfect, but deeply profound. Words mean things. Words mean something. The words we use (and of course how we use them) are far more powerful than we ever are willing to realize. It is more than just semantics; the words we use communicate important ideas, feelings and truths. Disappointment, guilt, shame, remorse, repentance and all the other words used in this book are not minor, nit-picky, issues of semantics; they are powerful forces we must understand. Words carry with them great meaning and power, and we must carefully consider the words we use, hear and apply to ourselves, as well as the truth they communicate. Do we say, hear and receive words that lift up the truth that is the Gospel of Jesus, or do we embrace words that communicate the powerful and painful lie that is the false gospel of guilt and shame? Words mean something—,in fact, they mean a lot. God is not disappointed in you. Not today, not yesterday, not ever. God loves us and wants the best for us, and God mourns when we feel pain and when we suffer— even though Jesus told us both would be a reality of life. God hurts when we hurt, even if we ourselves are the one causing the hurt we are experiencing. God loves us, God is not disappointed in us.

When it comes to the emotional response and ultimately, the emotional outcome of the story we choose to embrace, there are two clear and distinct paths. The first is the path of the evil one, and it is a lie. It is the path that comes when we choose to believe and embrace the false gospel of guilt and shame. The outcome of embracing the lie that is the false gospel of guilt and shame is simple: pain.

Now, I have yet to meet anyone who really loves pain. We all have different pain tolerances, physically and emotionally. C.S. Lewis notes that pain is a megaphone.[16] Pain tells us that something is not right, not as it should be. Pain, though unpleasant, is a good thing.

In the Bible, several stories describe people who have a disease called leprosy. It is marked by sores, open wounds, scabs, lost limbs and an assortment of other debilitating issues. One of the things leprosy can do is remove the ability to feel pain as it attacks the nerves. Many of the wounds those with this disease might have had resulted from getting injured and not knowing it. This past year I have had two knee surgeries and am preparing for a third. This is all due to a genetic condition. My most recent surgery included multiple procedures in one, and was basically a reconstruction of my right knee. As it continues to heal (and it is quite the journey) there are spots on my leg where my nerves have not fully regenerated. This is normal, and may or may not correct itself in every part of my leg. In those places where this is still an issue, I can feel very little. In fact, without already knowing something is touching those spots, all I can really feel is pressure. I do not have any sensation or pain. A month ago, I felt a strange sensation midway between my ankle and the area around my knee where I still do not have full feeling. I looked down and there was a small spot of blood dripping down my leg. I had cut my leg in the spot where I do not have feeling and because I did not feel it, I had no idea. I continue to get some small cuts and scrapes in those areas, since I just do not feel anything.

This insignificant issue been a powerful teacher for me. First, it is a constant reminder of what those with leprosy in

---

[16] Lewis C.S. *The Problem of Pain* (New York, NY: HarperCollins, 1996), 91.

Jesus' day must have experienced. They were covered in wounds and it was not their fault, yet they were so disgusting to look at and so feared that they were often forced to live in leper colonies outside the city limits. Secondly, it has reminded me of how important, helpful and necessary pain can be, though I do not enjoy it at all. Everyone has a different threshold for pain and we all hate pain, yet it does have value. Pain is a teacher.

If pain is important and necessary, yet unpleasant and hated, why is it such an important issue in terms of our emotional health? Is the emotional pain that is the result and outcome from embracing the false gospel of guilt and shame really a bad thing? The simple answer is yes. The pain that comes from embracing the lie of guilt and shame is a different kind of pain. It is not the temporary kind of necessary pain that is educational and helpful. Instead, the emotional pain that is a result of guilt and shame is perpetual. It never ends. While in light of my own experience and my understanding of leprosy I am thankful for pain, it is not something I want to live in and with constantly. While suffering and pain are a part of life that Jesus told us we would experience and should embrace, Jesus never intended for us to live in perpetual emotional pain. In fact, he died so we would not have to do so.

The perpetual emotional pain that comes from embracing guilt and shame is unhealthy, toxic and never-ending. It festers and grows, feeding off our guilt and shame and is characterized by an emotional pain that serves to continually punish us emotionally. Embracing guilt and shame is the same emotionally as it would be physically to pick up a baseball bat and continually hit ourselves with it, only hitting more often and with more force as the pain increases until we know nothing other than the pain. The emotional pain that comes from living in guilt and shame is a toxic cycle of emotional pain. It is emotional self-abuse.

The second path is the path of truth. It is the path of God, the Gospel of Jesus, the story of God's unconditional love and grace for everyone one of us in each and every moment of our lives. This path is marked not by perpetual emotional pain, but by emotional wholeness. In the end, what God desires for all people is wholeness: physically, emotionally, financially, relationally and spiritually. God wants us to be whole. God wants you to be whole. That is what you were created to be. It is what Jesus died to ensure. It is your destiny; it is my destiny. We were made to be whole, to be free, to be ourselves. God's only desire for us is all that is good. While we may experience pain and suffering, God does not want us to live in our pain and suffering, but rather desires to make us whole in the midst of it. When we embrace the Gospel of Jesus, we will still experience pain and suffering, but we will have the God of universe by our side, helping us to find, experience and live in wholeness. The outcome of the Gospel of Jesus is not perpetual emotional pain; rather, it is emotional wholeness in the midst of the pain we may experience as a part of life.

This second path, the path of God and truth, is centered on emotional wholeness, but it is also rooted in forgiveness. Forgiveness is not easy, and we all have a threshold for what is easy to forgive and what is not easy to forgive. Forgiving those who hurt us and those we love is not easy, but forgiveness is a requirement of following Jesus, of being a Christian. Forgiveness is also necessary for emotional health and wholeness. When we fail to forgive, we are allowing those who hurt us to live rent-free in our heads. When we do not seek to forgive, we continue to be hurt and to carry burden and pain. Unforgiveness does not hurt those who have done wrong; it hurts those who continue to live in it.

While forgiveness—especially the forgiveness of others—is a huge and important issue, it is not one I can adequately dissect in this book. That said, the issue of forgiveness as it relates to the false gospel of guilt and shame is not really about forgiving God or others, but it is forgiving ourselves. Much like the greatest commandment calls us to love God, others and ourselves, we also must find ways to forgive God, others and ourselves.

If I am transparent, I have to admit it is far easier for me to forgive God for something I experience than it is to forgive others. If I am really honest, it is almost always easier to forgive someone else than it is to forgive myself. When I fail to forgive myself, I am embracing the false gospel of guilt and shame. When I embrace guilt and shame, I refuse to forgive myself. Emotional healing and wholeness is not possible short- or long-term without self-forgiveness. Self-hatred and the failure to forgive ourselves are the fuels on which guilt and shame often run, and the evil one finds great delight when we refuse to forgive ourselves for our sins, mistakes and shortcomings. We must forgive ourselves when we fail, sin or make a mistake. There is no other way. For emotional health and freedom, and in order to fully embrace the Gospel of God's unconditional love and grace, we must forgive ourselves.

Our emotional health impacts our physical, spiritual and relational health far more than we realize. There are plenty of examples, research and life experiences which, if we are honest, demonstrate the tremendous power emotional health has over our lives. We often embrace a separation of heart and mind, emotional and intellect, but this is, in fact, physically and spiritually impossible. It is a contradiction of how we are created; it is not a biblical perspective in any way. The truth is that Jesus cares about every aspect of our lives and desires health and wholeness for each of us. Jesus desires for us to have life and have it to its fullest, and to have the freedom to be ourselves and the joy of abundant life. Our emotional health, the health of our hearts and how we feel matter greatly to God. The great tragedy of the false gospel of guilt and shame is the tremendous amount of damage it does to our emotional health, which effects every area of our lives. Choose emotional health. Choose the Gospel of Jesus. Choose forgiveness. Reject the evil one. Reject the lie that is the false gospel of guilt and shame.

Important Things to Remember from Chapter 9:

- God is not disappointed in you.

- When it comes to the emotional response and ultimately the emotional outcome of the story we choose to embrace, there are two clear and distinct paths. The first is the path of the evil one; it is a lie. It is the path that comes when we choose to believe and embrace the false gospel of guilt and shame. The outcome of embracing the lie that is the false gospel of guilt and shame is simple: pain.

- The perpetual emotional pain that comes from embracing guilt and shame is unhealthy, it is toxic and it never goes away. It festers and grows, feeding off our guilt and shame. The emotional pain that comes from embracing the false gospel of guilt and shame is characterized by an emotional pain that serves to continue to punish us emotionally.

- When you embrace the Gospel of Jesus, you will still experience pain and suffering, but you will have the God of the universe by your side, helping you to find, experience and live in wholeness.

- Emotional healing and wholeness are not possible short- or long-term without self-forgiveness. Self-hatred and the failure to forgive yourself is the fuel on which guilt and shame often run, and the evil one finds great delight when you refuse to forgive yourself for your sins, mistakes and shortcomings.

CHAPTER 10: DISCIPLE TO LEARN FROM: PETER VS. JUDAS

One of the better of my few original thoughts came almost a decade ago. As I was reading a familiar story in the New Testament, I realized there are some very important similarities between two of the characters of the New Testament who seem to have almost nothing in common: Peter and Judas. As I have studied these two disciples over time, I have noticed some important truths from their lives, especially as they relate to the false gospel of guilt and shame. In fact, these two disciples each represent the two competing narratives of our lives, the narrative of guilt and shame and the narrative of God's unconditional love and grace. These two disciples, Jesus' closest followers and friends, each have much to teach us when it comes to the false gospel of guilt and shame and the Gospel of Jesus, the truth of God's unconditional love and grace.

First, let us take a look at these two disciples by considering what they had in common. Both were part of the original 12 disciples called by Jesus. They were his core group that traveled and did ministry with him for three years. They lived together during that entire time and were a community. They were brothers and friends. Both Peter and Judas were full of potential, and that is why Jesus called them. They were both employed and left their livelihoods to follow Jesus. They embraced his teachings and recognized Jesus as the Messiah, the son of God.

They more than believed in Jesus; they gave up everything to follow him. Their entire lives became dedicated to his work, mission and ministry. They were both leaders; Judas and Peter were both essential to the movement of Jesus that would become the Christian church across the world we know today. It all started with Jesus and the Twelve. They were disciples who made disciples. Yet, neither Peter nor Judas were perfect. What we know suggests that both were pretty strong individuals with strong opinions. Both seemed to demonstrate some level of impulsiveness and some level of planning, with perhaps Peter being slightly more impulsive and Judas more of a planner. Peter and Judas are examined very differently today, but they had much in common.

Peter and Judas were also different in many ways: Peter, a fisherman, and Judas, a tax collector. One a blue-collar worker, the other more of a white-collar worker. One more trusted and likely more down to earth, the other, Judas, more influential and powerful. Peter was likely more rough around the edges and certainly a bit less formal and proper. Judas was more than an accountant or bean counter. As a tax collector, he was likely corrupt and dishonest. Tax collectors in that time were despised in a way we cannot always relate to. He likely had much more than Peter, but both in following Jesus put their livelihood aside and sacrificed both the good and bad of their reputations.

Peter emerged as one of the stronger leaders of the group and was quite impulsive, often speaking before thinking. Judas was much more calculating, and probably felt more like an outsider and less like a leader. Peter was likely used to discomfort and uncertainly; where Judas would be more likely to struggle in that way. Both intended to do good, but in the end, they both failed. Two entirely different men, following the same Jesus. Two men with a story that would later converge, then go in entirely different directions.

There is something else that both Peter and Judas had in common, something more significant than anything already mentioned. Peter and Judas both betrayed Jesus. Sure, they betrayed Jesus in different ways, but they both betrayed Jesus nonetheless. Consider their stories of betrayal:

Peter, after the arrest of Jesus:

> They took Jesus to the high priest, and all the chief priests, the elders and the teachers of the law came together. Peter followed him at a distance, right into the courtyard of the high priest. There he sat with the guards and warmed himself at the fire. The chief priests and the whole Sanhedrin were looking for evidence against Jesus so that they could put him to death, but they did not find any. Many testified falsely against him, but their statements did not agree. Then some stood up and gave this false testimony against him: "We heard him say, 'I will destroy this temple made with human hands and in three days will build another, not made with hands.'" Yet even then their testimony did not agree. Then the high priest stood up before them and asked Jesus, "Are you not going

to answer? What is this testimony that these men are bringing against you?" But Jesus remained silent and gave no answer. Again the high priest asked him, "Are you the Messiah, the Son of the Blessed One?" "I am," said Jesus. "And you will see the Son of Man sitting at the right hand of the Mighty One and coming on the clouds of heaven." The high priest tore his clothes. "Why do we need any more witnesses?" he asked. "You have heard the blasphemy. What do you think?" They all condemned him as worthy of death. Then some began to spit at him; they blindfolded him, struck him with their fists, and said, "Prophesy!" And the guards took him and beat him. While Peter was below in the courtyard, one of the servant girls of the high priest came by. When she saw Peter warming himself, she looked closely at him. "You also were with that Nazarene, Jesus," she said. But he denied it. "I don't know or understand what you're talking about," he said, and went out into the entryway. When the servant girl saw him there, she said again to those standing around, "This fellow is one of them." Again he denied it. After a little while, those standing near said to Peter, "Surely you are one of them, for you are a Galilean." He began to call down curses, and he swore to them, "I don't know this man you're talking about." Immediately the rooster crowed the second time. Then Peter remembered the words Jesus had spoken to him: "Before the rooster crows twice you will disown me three times." And he broke down and wept. [17]

---

[17] Mark 14:53-72 *NIV*

Judas, in the arrest of Jesus:

> Then one of the Twelve—the one called Judas Iscariot—went to the chief priests and asked, "What are you willing to give me if I deliver him over to you?" So they counted out for him thirty pieces of silver. From then on Judas watched for an opportunity to hand him over. [18] While he was still speaking, Judas, one of the Twelve, arrived. With him was a large crowd armed with swords and clubs, sent from the chief priests and the elders of the people. Now the betrayer had arranged a signal with them: "The one I kiss is the man; arrest him." Going at once to Jesus, Judas said, "Greetings, Rabbi!" and kissed him. Jesus replied, "Do what you came for, friend." Then the men stepped forward, seized Jesus and arrested him.[19]

Jesus predicted both betrayals:

> When evening came, Jesus was reclining at the table with the Twelve. And while they were eating, he said, "Truly I tell you, one of you will betray me." They were very sad and began to say to him one after the other, "Surely you don't mean me, Lord?" Jesus replied, "The one who has dipped his hand into the bowl with me will betray me. The Son of Man will go just as it is written about him. But woe to that man who betrays the Son of Man! It would be better for him if he had not been born." Then Judas, the one

---

[18] Matthew 26:14-16 *NIV*
[19] Matthew 26:47-50 *NIV*

who would betray him, said, "Surely you don't mean me, Rabbi?" Jesus answered, "You have said so."[20]

Then Jesus told them, "This very night you will all fall away on account of me, for it is written: "'I will strike the shepherd, and the sheep of the flock will be scattered.' But after I have risen, I will go ahead of you into Galilee." Peter replied, "Even if all fall away on account of you, I never will." "Truly I tell you," Jesus answered, "this very night, before the rooster crows, you will disown me three times." But Peter declared, "Even if I have to die with you, I will never disown you." And all the other disciples said the same.[21]

There is also a related and important difference between Peter and Judas, something that most people miss but is very powerful. While both betrayed Jesus, the most important difference in Peter and Judas was their response after they betrayed Jesus. Consider their stories:

Afterward Jesus appeared again to his disciples, by the Sea of Galilee. It happened this way: Simon Peter, Thomas (also known as Didymus), Nathanael from Cana in Galilee, the sons of Zebedee, and two other disciples were together. "I'm going out to fish," Simon Peter told them, and they said, "We'll go with you." So they went out and got into the boat, but that night they caught nothing. Early in the morning, Jesus stood on the shore, but the disciples did not realize that it was Jesus. He called out to them, "Friends, haven't you any fish?" "No," they

---

[20] Matthew 26:20-25 *NIV*
[21] Matthew 26:31-35 *NIV*

answered. He said, "Throw your net on the right side of the boat and you will find some." When they did, they were unable to haul the net in because of the large number of fish. Then the disciple whom Jesus loved said to Peter, "It is the Lord!" As soon as Simon Peter heard him say, "It is the Lord," he wrapped his outer garment around him (for he had taken it off) and jumped into the water. The other disciples followed in the boat, towing the net full of fish, for they were not far from shore, about a hundred yards. When they landed, they saw a fire of burning coals there with fish on it, and some bread.[22]

Early in the morning, all the chief priests and the elders of the people made their plans how to have Jesus executed. So they bound him, led him away and handed him over to Pilate the governor. When Judas, who had betrayed him, saw that Jesus was condemned, he was seized with remorse and returned the thirty pieces of silver to the chief priests and the elders. "I have sinned," he said, "for I have betrayed innocent blood." "What is that to us?" they replied. "That's your responsibility." So Judas threw the money into the temple and left. Then he went away and hanged himself.[23]

Reflecting on these two disciples and their stories, I continue to look to the significant thing they have in common, their betrayal of Jesus. I am struck that each in his own way denied, rejected, betrayed and disowned Jesus. Judas for some coins sold Jesus out to the authorities.

---

[22] John 21:1-9 NIV
[23] Matthew 27:1-3 NIV

Peter, the one who said he would never betray Jesus, denied him three times, all likely within hearing distance of him. After following Jesus and doing life and ministry together for three years, both these men, filled with potential, betrayed Jesus.

What is interesting is that today, more than 2,000 years later, we look at one as a bit of a hero and the other as most certainly a villain. In fact, the name Judas, or Judas Iscariot, has been used as an insult for one who betrays someone, sells someone out. Peter, in church history and in the words of Jesus, becomes the rock, the foundation upon which the church is built, a hero and leader. How is it that these two disciples, both whom failed and betrayed Jesus, can be seen so differently? Sure, Peter's betrayal was just words and Judas' betrayal led to the arrest of Jesus, but are not both betrayals deeply painful rejections that came from trusted friends?

In the end, the most significant difference between these two disciples, their story and their legacies is found in their response to their denial of Jesus, their reaction and responses to their sin and failure. Judas gave up. Filled with pain, guilt and shame, he went and took his own life, committed suicide by hanging himself in the midst of his failure and despair. He saw no hope, no way out, no forgiveness, no way forward.

Peter, on the other hand, does something entirely different and finds forgiveness, restoration, healing and wholeness. Peter, in the midst of his sin and failure when he sees Jesus, runs to Jesus. In fact, he cannot even wait for the boat to move a short distance to shore; instead, he jumps out of the boat and swims to Jesus. This moment is interesting and profound. To be honest, if I had betrayed the son of God and denied him to others in front of him three times,

I am not sure my first instinct would be to run toward the son of God who could calm the sea and walk on water!

Peter, in his slightly impulsive response, gets something much deeper. He understands something deeper that Judas missed, which we often miss also. What matters most is not who, how or in what way we sin or fail. What matters is the direction we run (or swim) when we sin, fail or make a mistake. At the end of the day, the most profound difference between Judas and Peter was the direction in which they ran when they failed Jesus, when they failed as disciples, when they rejected the God who loved them without condition. Judas ran away; Peter ran toward Jesus. In the end, that one action is what distinguishes the legacy of the leader and hero in Peter and the villain in Judas. In the end, Peter found victory, healing, wholeness, unconditional love and grace. Judas found despair, pain, rejection and death.

The false gospel of guilt and shame has a character, a disciple and a face, and that face is Judas. The truth found in the Gospel of Jesus also has a character, a disciple and a face, and that face is Peter. Two ordinary men. Two imperfect disciples trying to follow Jesus. Two people who betrayed Jesus, who both sinned and failed greatly and publicly. Peter's life ended in joy and victory. Peter's story culminates with the forgiveness and restoration he receives from Jesus on the shore of the lake, the story of remorse and repentance. Judas story culminates with isolation, death and despair, the story of guilt and shame.

The Gospel of Jesus leads us to a life of wholeness, a life of freedom and love with Jesus, where in the midst of our sins, mistakes and shortcomings, we can find healing, restoration and wholeness. The false gospel of guilt and shame however, leads us to a life of loneliness and despair, a life without unconditional love and grace, a life filled with guilt and shame. A life that leads in the end to death.

I sin. I make mistakes. I have shortcomings. I do not meet the standards of the Scriptures, my own standards and the standards of those I care about on a regular basis. I succeed and I fail, sometimes intentionally and sometimes not. In the end, what carries the most significance is not the way in which I sin, fail or fall short, but the direction I run afterward. There remain two competing narratives in the world, two competing narratives in our lives, two narratives that compete for our heart. There is the Gospel of Jesus and the truth of the unconditional love and grace of God, and there is the lie crafted by the evil one, the false gospel of guilt and shame. We have a choice. We choose which narrative to believe, which narrative to embrace. Much like Peter and Judas, when we fail, we have a choice. Will we take the path of truth and life and run to Jesus, or will we take the path of guilt and shame, the path that ends in death?

Important Things to Remember from Chapter 10:

- As we study these two characters (Peter and Judas), we notice some important truths from their lives, especially as they relate to the false gospel of guilt and shame. In fact, these two disciples each represent the two competing narratives of our lives, the narrative of guilt and shame and the narrative of God's unconditional love and grace.

- In the end, the most significant difference between these two disciples, their stories and their legacies is found in their response to their denial of Jesus, their reactions and responses to their sin and failure. Judas gave up. Filled with pain, guilt and shame, he took his own life, committing suicide by hanging himself in the midst of his failure and despair. Peter, in the midst of his sin and failure, when he sees Jesus, runs to him.

- Reflecting on these two disciples, we see the significant thing they have in common: both betrayed Jesus. Each in his own way denied, rejected, betrayed and disowned Jesus. Judas sold Jesus out to the authorities for some coins. Peter, the one who said he would never betray Jesus, denied him three times, all likely within hearing distance of him.

- The false gospel of guilt and shame has a character, a disciple and a face: Judas. The truth found in the Gospel of Jesus, God's unconditional love and grace, also has a character, a disciple and a face: Peter. Two ordinary men. Two imperfect disciples trying to follow Jesus. Two people who betrayed Jesus, who both sinned and failed greatly and publicly. Peter's life ended in joy and victory. Peter's story culminates with the forgiveness and restoration he receives from Jesus on the shore of the lake. Judas' story culminates with isolation, death and despair.

- There remain two competing narratives in the world, two competing narratives in our lives, two narratives that compete for our heart. There is the Gospel of Jesus and the truth of the unconditional love and grace of God, and there is the lie crafted by the evil one, the false gospel of guilt and shame. We have a choice. We choose which narrative to believe, which narrative to embrace.

CHAPTER 11: THEOLOGY: COMPELLED OR CONDEMNED?

While there are many factors at play in guilt and shame, emotionally and otherwise, important theological concepts also lie in both narratives. While there are many things to think about theologically as it relates to guilt and shame that are woven throughout this book, there are two key competing theological principles that must be examined in order to understand and conquer guilt and shame. The false gospel of guilt and shame is rooted in the theological principle of condemnation. The Gospel of Jesus is rooted in the theological concept of being compelled.

For most people, the first thought we have when we sin, make a mistake or are dealing with one of our shortcomings is focused on ourselves. There is something natural about thinking first about yourself when you have failed, and while it is not ideal, it is normal and natural. We think about what went wrong, what could have been different. We think about what happens next and wrestle with why we have failed. We often dwell in our failure, focusing not on the good or positive, but on the bad, the negative. This is also human instinct, but is neither healthy nor effective. We must be realistic and honest; we are not called to live in denial, but neither can we live in negativity.

The key is moving from the first thought about ourselves and moving beyond that to focus on truth, a focus on God. The key is to focus on who we are in Jesus, how God sees us, and not focusing on who we are in the midst of sin, failure or shortcomings. We have to move from the first thought of ourselves in our sin and move to thinking about and focusing on how we can be healed, redeemed and made whole in Jesus. Rather than seeing ourselves through the lens of our shortcomings, we must see ourselves through the lens of Jesus, that we are a chosen, beloved child with whom he is well-pleased.

The idea of condemnation is fairly simple. It means we are destined for death and destruction, and there is no hope, no rescue, nothing we can do about it. It is full of despair, judgment, anger and hatred. To be condemned is to be sentenced, to be punished. Condemnation brings with it a sense of finality. To be condemned is to be rejected, not only for performance, but for identity as well. It is a complete rejection of love and grace and denies the existence of any self-worth or value. The false gospel of guilt and shame is rooted in condemnation. Condemnation is rooted entirely in our performance and allows for no room for improvement, reconciliation, forgiveness or healing. It is miserable, lonely and hopeless. Condemnation is not of God.

In Jesus, we receive the promise that there is no condemnation for those who embrace Jesus. Jesus offers us a life free of condemnation; the evil one and the lie of guilt and shame bring only a lifetime of condemnation. Not only is condemnation at the root of the false gospel of guilt and shame, it is the result and the sentence that come from living in the lie of guilt and shame. This may well be the very definition of hell, to live in constant condemnation, to live in guilt and shame with absolutely no hope.

The key and opposite theological value that is at the root of the Gospel of Jesus is the concept of being compelled. So often, people think of Jesus as fire insurance, that he exists to save us from hell after we die. Many churches teach this. While there is certainly truth to this statement, it is at best only a small piece of the story. Jesus did not just come to save us from hell, to save us *from* something, but to save us *to* something. We focus so much on what happens after we die that we truly fail to live. Of course, saving us for eternity was a significant part of the mission of Jesus, but Jesus also came to show us how to have abundant life now, how to live in the here and now. Those who reject the false gospel of guilt and shame and embrace the Gospel of Jesus are compelled. They are compelled to live differently, to live freely, to live in God's unconditional love and grace.

The Gospel of Jesus isn't just about life after we die; it is about our life now, today, each and every day. In the Gospel of Jesus, we are compelled to live a life of joy, hope and freedom. We are compelled to see the world differently than the culture around us; rather than focusing on fear, division, guilt and shame, we are called to a life of hope, trust, love and grace.

Living under the concept of being compelled means having freedom to be yourself, to live a joyful, abundant life and to live in hope, not in fear or condemnation. Freedom comes "when we are whole and fully self-accepting," and when we have this freedom, "we have the freedom to see and hear what see and hear, rather than what we should or should not see and hear."²⁴ When we embrace self-acceptance and embrace the Gospel of Jesus, we are able to choose the voices that we give power to in our lives. When we get trapped in the false gospel of guilt and shame, we are trapped into listening to only the negative, condemning voices. In the Gospel of Jesus we know that our sins, mistakes and shortcomings are not the whole story and are never the end of the story. "Self-acceptance overcomes the self-rupture of toxic shame."²⁵ So often it is much easier to be and feel like the victim than to embrace hope, but the harder way is often the best way, and in this case, it is the way to wholeness and life abundant.

There is a timeless illustration involving a glass of water. Half of the glass is full; half of it is empty. The illustration points out that the optimist sees the glass as half full while the pessimist sees it as half empty. This is accurate and helpful, but incomplete. I think there are two other types of people who will look at this glass in different ways. The realist states that it is a glass and it has water in it. The Christian sees the glass as refillable. Perspective is a powerful thing. We often function in two extremes, over-focusing on reality or denying it completely. We get caught up on being entirely negative and pessimistic or overly positive and optimistic. Both have value, but our focus must be on moving forward, on hope. Rather than trying to be a pessimist, optimist or realist, we can embrace the value of each and put our energy in recognizing and living in the truth that the glass is refillable. In Jesus we find hope, restoration, healing and redemption. The story does not

---

[24] Bradshaw John, *Healing the Shame that Binds You* (Deerfield Beach, FL: Health Communications, Inc., 2005), 154.
[25] Bradshaw John, *Healing the Shame that Binds You* (Deerfield Beach, FL: Health Communications, Inc., 2005), 154.

end with a glass that has water in it, whether it is half full or half empty.

The question we must ask ourselves is, are we condemned or compelled? Do we embrace the condemnation found in the false gospel of guilt and shame, or do we choose to embrace the truth that we are no longer condemned in Jesus and are compelled to a greater, more free, abundant life? The condemnation found in guilt and shame leads to despair and death; it is hopeless. The joy found in being compelled by Jesus to live in freedom, to live as Christ calls us to live, brings great life. Are we condemned or are we compelled?

Important Things to Remember from Chapter 11:

- The false gospel of guilt and shame is rooted in the theological principle of condemnation. The Gospel of Jesus is rooted in the theological concept of being compelled.

- Not only is condemnation at the root of the false gospel of guilt and shame, it is the result and sentence that comes from living in the lies of guilt and shame. This may well be the very definition of hell, to live in constant condemnation, to live in guilt and shame with absolutely no hope.

- Those who reject the false gospel of guilt and shame and embrace the Gospel of Jesus are compelled. They are compelled to live differently, to live freely, to live in God's unconditional love and grace. The Gospel of Jesus is not just about life after we die, it is about our lives now, today, each and every day. In the Gospel of Jesus we are compelled to live a life of joy, hope and freedom.

- There is a timeless illustration involving a glass of water. Half of the glass is full, half of it is empty. The illustration points out that the optimist sees the glass as half full while the pessimist sees it as half empty. This is accurate and helpful, but incomplete. Two other types of people will look at this glass in different ways. The realist states it is a glass and has water in it. The Christian sees the glass as refillable. Perspective is a powerful thing.

- The condemnation found in guilt and shame leads to despair and death; it is hopeless. The joy found in being compelled by Jesus to live in freedom, to live as

Christ calls you to live, brings great life. Are you condemned or are you compelled?

CHAPTER 12: GOSPEL: LOVE, MERCY AND GRACE VS. NOTHING

The word Gospel refers to the teachings of Jesus, both through his words and his actions. The idea of a gospel (small g) is a meta-narrative or bigger picture story that answers the key questions of life. Again, in this book we are discussing the truth of the Gospel of Jesus and the false gospel (small g) of guilt and shame. The word "gospel" has a root meaning of "good news." Most followers of Jesus easily forget the Gospel of Jesus is good news! We tend to be more bad news people, at least in the United States today. The Gospel of Jesus is all good news, no bad news at all. One of the key signs the false gospel of guilt and shame is in fact a false gospel is that there is absolutely no good news to it at all.

Story is a very powerful thing. We don't realize it, but story is everywhere. We tell stories every day. We see stories in movies and television shows. We find stories in newspapers and magazines. The internet is full of stories. Social media is filled with personal stories in posts, links to stories and more. We hear stories in music; see stories in art. Marketers are constantly trying to tell us a story when they sell us a product. Sports are filled with stories. Dramas, plays and musicals are all stories. Comedy often tells us a story, as does tragedy. When we reflect on our lives, we see stories all around us. Life is one big story made up of many smaller stories. The Bible is the big story of God and God's relationship with us and the world filled with many important stories. Stories are sacred.

Not all stories are equal, however. Some stories carry varying meaning depending on who is telling the story, who is hearing the story and how the story is told. Stories vary in their level of truth. Stories vary by culture and are interpreted differently by race, gender, economic class, generation and other factors. While many would like to believe truth is a moving target, people don't genuinely believe this about everything in their lives. Most people can agree that things like child abuse, rape and murder are wrong. We accept these things as truth. Contrast that with our political culture and we see how differently we can view truth. One side may see the action of the opposing side as immoral and wrong when just a day prior they were defending someone on their side from the very same thing, saying that in their case it was not wrong.

Still, at the end of the day, truth does exist and while we do not always agree on what that is, it exists and it does not change based on our thoughts or feelings. We come to know things as true by facts, but not by facts alone. We cannot know truth without facts either. Truth is something we know, believe, understand and experience, much like story. A gospel story is a story that tries to communicate truth. The Gospel of Jesus is a story I believe to be true. I know it intellectually, historically, emotionally, spiritually and relationally. While I might have differing beliefs about various aspects of faith from the person next door, I choose to embrace the Gospel of Jesus, the truth of God's unconditional love and grace as just that: truth.

We are led to believe that the false gospel of guilt and shame is not in fact false, but is the truth. Furthermore, we are often led to believe that the gospel of guilt and shame is a part of the Gospel of Jesus, which could not be further from the truth. It is this challenge and the resulting confusion, pain and despair that has inspired this book. Guilt and shame are not of God. They have no part in or anything to do with the Gospel of Jesus, the good news. Guilt and shame are of the evil one. It is not good news and brings nothing good or healthy. When we get to the heart of what the Gospel of Jesus communicates and gives us and what the false gospel of guilt and shame communicates and give us, we see a clear, simple, yet stark contrast in two competing stories.

In the Gospel of Jesus, we find many important smaller stories and truths. When contrasted against the false gospel of guilt and shame, there are three primary truths, three pieces of good news that stand out. First, is the principle and truth of love. Love trumps everything. If I were to sum up Christianity, Jesus or the Gospel in one word, it would be love. Love always wins. Love is the supreme value and the most significant truth of the Gospel of Jesus. Love does not fail; love is filled with hope. Love covers and transcends everything.

That is why when Jesus was asked what was the greatest of all the commandments, laws and rules, he responded with love. Love God with everything you have, love others with everything you have and are and love yourself. All the rules, laws, commandments and moral codes that could ever exist are fulfilled when we focus on love. The opposite of love is not always hate; more often it is fear. Love is completely absent from the false gospel of guilt and shame. Instead, guilt and shame focus on fear and self-hatred, the antithesis of love.

The second value of significance in the Gospel of Jesus as it relates to guilt and shame is mercy. Mercy is an emphasis in the teaching, ministry and life of Jesus. We have lost sight of the value of mercy in our culture, focusing on justice, revenge and division. That is what the false gospel of guilt and shame does. It centers our focus on ourselves and our need for justice and revenge. It feeds the division and fear that are suffocating our world today. Guilt and shame are focused on the negative aspects of our performance, the places where we do not measure up. Mercy leads us to value and love others in spite of their sins, mistakes and shortcomings. Mercy leads us to love and value others in spite of our disagreements and differences. Mercy leads us to know that we have great value regardless of our imperfections. Mercy is the way of Jesus. Mercy is not the way of the evil one. There is no room for mercy for others or oneself in the false gospel of guilt and shame.

The third and final contrasting value is grace. Again, grace is God's unmerited favor. It is the opposite of karma. In karma, everyone is punished in some way, because we all sin, make mistakes and have shortcomings. In grace, we are able to move beyond our sin, mistakes and shortcomings regardless of the pain and suffering that may come from the natural consequences of these failures. Grace is a gift, but like all gifts it must be accepted, it must be desired and it must be embraced. Grace means that with the help of God, everything is going to work out; grace means there is forgiveness and hope.

Whatever challenges you may face, those challenges along with your sins, mistakes and shortcomings are not the end of the story. They are not the full story. In grace, we are measured by our value as people created in the image of God: unique, gifted and beautiful, loved and capable of love. In grace, we are seen as worthy as beloved children of God. In grace, we are worthy because we are children of God who are loved, chosen and adopted. In grace, we accept our identity as a loved child of God with whom God is well pleased.

The challenge is not understanding or believing grace, but embracing grace. Guilt and shame are the greatest roadblocks to embracing grace. One of the greatest weapons against guilt and shame is to make grace personal. The more personal grace becomes, the more guilt and shame are crowded out of our lives. The more personal grace becomes for us, the less personal everything else will feel. Choose grace. "When we are loved unconditionally, i.e., accepted just as we are, we can then accept ourselves just as we are."[26] This is the power of God's grace and unconditional, no-strings-attached love.

In the false gospel of guilt and shame, there is no love, mercy or grace. They are completely absent. In fact, in the false gospel of guilt in shame there is nothing good, no good news at all. It is a false gospel, a perversion of the truth and an insult to love. When we look at the good values that come from guilt and shame, the helpful and healthy things that come from guilt and shame, we find none. Again, do not confuse guilt and shame with repentance and remorse, where we learn from our sin and mistakes. In guilt and shame, we *are* our sin and mistakes—there is no truth, there is no good news, there is no life. There is nothing of God in guilt and shame, not a single thing. It is a destructive, manipulative, demeaning, isolating and toxic lie. It is to be rejected at every turn. It is a fight

---

[26] Bradshaw John, *Healing the Shame that Binds You* (Deerfield Beach, FL: Health Communications, Inc., 2005), 154.

that is not always easy, but always worth fighting. Our hearts, our relationships and our lives are too valuable to allow guilt and shame to steal, kill and destroy all that is good in us.

Which path do you choose in the midst of sin/failure? Which direction do you run when you fail God, those you love or yourself? Are you going to choose the way of Peter or the way of Jesus? Will you choose the fullness of love, mercy and grace or the emptiness of guilt and shame? Will you choose the Gospel of Jesus or the false gospel of guilt and shame? We do have a choice when we fail, sin or fall short. We can choose the path of truth, love and grace or the path of destruction. Run from shame and refuse to shame others. Embrace the Gospel of Jesus.

Important Things to Remember from Chapter 12:

- Story is a very powerful thing. We do not realize it, but story is everywhere. We tell stories every day. Not all stories are equal, however. Some stories carry varying meanings depending on who is telling the story, who is hearing the story and how the story is told. Stories vary in their level of truth.

- We are led to believe the false gospel of guilt and shame is not in fact false, but is the truth. Furthermore, we are often led to believe the gospel of guilt and shame is a part of the Gospel of Jesus, which could not be further from the truth.

- When contrasted against the false gospel of guilt and shame, there are three primary truths, three pieces of good news that stand out. Love trumps everything. If I were to sum up Christianity, Jesus or the Gospel in one word, it would be love. Mercy leads us to value and love others in spite of their sins, mistakes and shortcomings. Mercy leads us to love and value others in spite of our disagreements and differences. Mercy leads us to know that we have great value regardless of our imperfections. Mercy is the way of Jesus. The third and final contrasting value is grace. Again, grace is God's unmerited favor.

- One of the greatest weapons against guilt and shame is to make grace personal. The more personal grace becomes, the more guilt and shame are crowded out of our lives. The more personal grace becomes for us, the less personal everything else will feel.

- There is nothing of God in guilt and shame, not a single thing. It is a destructive, manipulative, demeaning, isolating, toxic lie. It is to be rejected at every turn. It is a fight that is not always easy, but always worth fighting. Our hearts, our relationships and our lives are too valuable to allow guilt and shame to steal, kill and destroy all that is good in us.

CHAPTER 13: SPIRITUAL RESULT: SPIRIT-FILLED LIFE VS. LEGALISM OR ABUSED FREEDOM

When it comes to human beings, everything is truly interconnected. Our emotional health impacts our physical health; our physical health impacts our emotional health. Subtle changes in stress levels can dramatically alter our sleep patterns. Our spiritual health has a tremendous impact on other areas of our life as well. In the same vein, our emotional health is deeply interconnected to our spiritual health, no matter what we might believe in terms of faith. When we look at the two paths discussed in this book, the Gospel of Jesus Christ and the false gospel of guilt and shame, there are two distinct spiritual results. In the end, addressing the false gospel of guilt and shame is all about health and wholeness.

When we embrace the false gospel of guilt and shame, there are one of two spiritual results: legalism or abused freedom. The word "result" is a bit deceiving, as it is more of a fluid outcome. One could be embracing the false gospel of guilt and shame and be stuck in legalism during a particular season of life, and then end up on the other end of the spectrum of abused freedom in another season. While the impact of guilt and shame is dramatic and significant, it does not have to be permanent—but far too often it is. When we are unhealthy in a spiritual sense, regardless of our faith or beliefs, it does have a significant impact on all aspects of our lives. Indeed, guilt and shame have the greatest impact on our emotional, relational and spiritual health. Despite this, we are created to be whole and healthy in every sense of the word. Guilt and shame steal life from us.

The first possible spiritual result or outcome of embracing the false gospel of guilt and shame is legalism. Legalism is rigid, draining and heretical. It is the modern-day equivalent of the religious Pharisees that Jesus challenged and criticized. In legalism, our life is structured entirely around rigid rules and obedience. This rigid obedience and observes of rules is something we impose upon others and upon ourselves when we embrace legalism.

Legalism is always an impossible standard. It is impossible, because it is not something we can achieve. It is impossible because we are imperfect. It is impossible, because we are sinners. It is impossible, because it is always a standard no one can meet. Legalism is rooted entirely in fear, and it is a desperate attempt to address fear through control. Legalism is not only unhealthy and unrealistic, it is also unbiblical. Legalism is the way of a Pharisee and not of a disciple of Jesus.

The idea of Christian legalism is a complete irony and falsehood. Not only is legalism contrary to the Gospel of Jesus Christ, it is also contrary to everything Jesus did and taught. Very few things angered Jesus more than legalism, and some of his sharpest and most critical words were for the Pharisees who lived and imposed a life of rigid legalism on everyone. Jesus came to fulfill the law so that legalism was no longer necessary. In his coming, life, death and resurrection, Jesus destroyed legalism by making it unnecessary. Jesus made it unnecessary out of love, and because it we can never measure up to legalism's. Jesus destroyed legalism because he loves all people deeply and does not want anyone to live in guilt, shame or legalism.

Legalism destroys our spiritual lives and highlights only our sin, tearing apart our identity as beloved, chosen, children of God. When we embrace guilt and shame, we feel a need to not only punish ourselves continually, but to compensate for our failures by creating an illusion of control when we impose an impossible set of standards upon ourselves. Guilt and shame create an internal sense of chaos in our lives, and the pain caused by guilt and shame cause us to feel out of control. This is why it is both a part of addiction cycles and why guilt and shame can lead to legalism. Legalism is used in a subconscious way to make us think that we do measure up in some way, which is a great irony because legalism ultimately only highlights our sin, mistakes and shortcomings. Legalism as a spiritual result or outcome completely dismisses the unconditional love and grace of God, much to the delight of the evil one.

The opposite negative spiritual result or outcome of embracing the false gospel of guilt and shame is abused freedom. This is where we see the spiritual impact of guilt and shame in terms of cycles of addiction. We can make two great mistakes with God's grace: we can choose to reject it (which is what legalism does) or we can choose to abuse it. Dietrich Bonhoeffer calls this "cheap grace," where we use grace as an excuse to do whatever we want, no matter how sinful or destructive to others or ourselves it may be. Guilt and shame often cause us to give up morally and spiritually. The way in which guilt and shame highlight our sin, mistakes and shortcomings often creates a strong and unhealthy reaction. This unhealthy reaction is to embrace a mindset that since we cannot measure up in anyway, we should not try. This is at the heart of abused freedom.

We were created to be free, and Jesus died for every human being so we could be free. Still, we are often confused about what freedom means, especially in the United States. Freedom is not about doing whatever we want and never having consequences. Freedom is about having choices and being free to fully be oneself, both in the American understanding and in the spiritual understanding of freedom. It seems we are constantly being told what we should do and who we should be. Family, friends, marketers, culture, government, employers, churches and many other people and groups are constantly communicating to us who and what we should be, creating yet another impossible standard to measure up to. Freedom means we get to choose what we believe and how we live. Freedom means we can choose to fit a mold imposed by someone or something else, or we can choose to fully be ourselves. One of the great challenges of guilt and shame is that it often causes us to believe we do not have that choice.

Abused freedom and cheap grace are the spiritual equivalent of an "anything goes" mentality. It is the equivalent of living internally and often externally, much like college students on a wild spring break with their friends, doing anything they want regardless of the impact or harm to self or others. This is the spiritual aspect of addiction where guilt and shame are present. We are free to do whatever we want, but not without impact or consequence to others or ourselves.

Jesus did not die so we could be free and have free will to do harmful things to ourselves and others, but rather so we could have the freedom to be ourselves and to be healthy and whole. Those who engage in addiction and harmful activities often struggle with guilt and shame; spiritually they are living in abused freedom. Many times they have given up and care little for themselves. Guilt and shame, while having the greatest impact on our emotional, relational and spiritual health, can impact our physical health greatly and that often comes through abused freedom. Guilt and shame cause irrational, unhealthy and toxic behavior that is deeply destructive.

When we embrace the Gospel of Jesus, even imperfectly and inconsistently, we end up with an entirely different spiritual result or outcome: we end up being fully free. It creates wholeness, abundance and joy. When we embrace the Gospel of Jesus and reject the false gospel of guilt and shame, we truly live the spirit-filled life. What is the spirit-filled life? It is a life centered on and full of the Holy Spirit. It is a life marked by freedom, joy and peace. It is a life of health and wholeness. It is also a life that naturally becomes marked with the fruit of the spirit.

> But the fruit of the Spirit is love, joy, peace, forbearance, kindness, goodness, faithfulness, gentleness and self-control. Against such things there is no law. Those who belong to Christ Jesus have crucified the flesh with its passions and desires. Since we live by the Spirit, let us keep in step with the Spirit.[27]

---

[27] Galatians 5:22-25 *NIV*

What is amazing about living in the Gospel of Jesus and rejecting guilt and shame is that over time we are changed, transformed, as we become more fully free and who we are created to be. As a result, life is changed in a way to create not only inward health, but a life that is overall healthy and good. Our transformation may help and impact others who are struggling with guilt and shame, among other things. It is not about an obligation to honor some moral code. It is instead living a free, healthy and whole life, devoid of destructive, unhealthy and harmful habits, actions and characteristics.

Guilt and shame are powerful forces in the world and in our lives. Guilt and shame impact many areas of our life, including our spiritual life and health regardless of our beliefs or faith perspectives. We were created to be free—free to choose, free to live, free to be ourselves. Guilt and shame distort and destroy that freedom, trapping us in legalism or an abuse of freedom often destructive to ourselves and others. Guilt and shame can only take away our freedom if we allow it to. There is another way, another narrative, another path. It is the Gospel of Jesus, the story of God's unconditional love and grace. It is the story that leads to true freedom and to health and wholeness. We can be free from the burden of guilt and shame, and it is that freedom for which Jesus died to offer to all humanity.

Important Things to Remember from Chapter 13:

- When we look at the two paths discussed in this book, the Gospel of Jesus Christ and the false gospel of guilt and shame, there are two distinct spiritual results. In the end, addressing the false gospel of guilt and shame is all about health and wholeness.

- Legalism is always an impossible standard, because it is not something that we can achieve. It is impossible, because we are imperfect. It is impossible, because we are sinners. Legalism is rooted entirely in fear and it is a desperate attempt to address fear through control.

- The opposite negative spiritual result or outcome of embracing the false gospel of guilt and shame is abused freedom. This is where we see the spiritual impact of guilt and shame in terms of cycles of addiction. We can make two great mistakes with God's grace: we can choose to reject it (which is what legalism does) or we can choose to abuse it.

- When we embrace the Gospel of Jesus, even imperfectly and inconsistently so, we end up with an entirely different spiritual result or outcome. When we embrace the Gospel of Jesus, spiritually we end up being fully free. It creates wholeness, abundance and joy.

- We were created to be free—free to choose, free to live, free to be ourselves. Guilt and shame distort and destroy that freedom, trapping us in legalism or an abuse of freedom often destructive to ourselves and others. Guilt and shame can only take away our freedom if we allow it to.

CHAPTER 14: THE ROLE OF GUILT AND SHAME

We have examined in great detail the problem of guilt and shame. We have looked at the various aspects of the two narratives, the false gospel of guilt and shame and the Gospel of Jesus. Guilt and shame are real, and they are toxic and destructive in many ways. The gospel of guilt and shame is a tool of the evil one and is destroying individuals, relationships and communities. Unfortunately, the false gospel of guilt and shame has infected our culture, communities and churches. While the problems with guilt and shame are many—and hopefully obvious at this point—overcoming guilt and shame is not an easy journey. It takes knowledge, effort, support and encouragement, and it is not a journey to walk alone.

It is often much easier to embrace guilt and shame than it is to embrace the no-strings-attached, unconditional love of God. Shaming is easy, yet forgiveness is hard. The false gospel of guilt and shame moves beyond momentary feelings of guilt and shame to something deeper. Under those circumstances, "Instead of the momentary feeling of being limited, making a mistake, littleness, or being less attractive or talented than someone else, a person can come to believe that his whole self is fundamentally flawed and defective."[28] This is the essence of the false gospel of guilt and shame, and it is fundamentally contradictory to the Gospel of Jesus Christ.

If the first step is identifying and understand the problem of guilt and shame, the second step is deciding to seek to both reject and overcome the false gospel of guilt and shame. This requires spiritual discernment. Bradshaw writes, "Spiritual discernment is our first line of defense against deception."[29] To help us understand this idea, "Discernment is that little 'buzzer' goes off inside when something is wrong."[30] It also requires an intentional decision. It is not just a one-time intentional decision, but a decision that must be made over and over again, because guilt and shame often reoccur and reemerge in the right situations and circumstances.

Do you really want to be free? Do you really want to be clean? Do you want to be healed? The answer to these questions may appear to be an obvious "yes," but when we really think about it, sometimes that is not the case. So often we are afraid of the work it takes to overcome things like guilt and shame. In some instances, we are so used to a problem we cannot imagine life without it, and we do not genuinely believe we can overcome it. Guilt and shame *can* be overcome and are not something we should accept or live with.

The third key to overcoming guilt and shame is allowing grace to become more personal. The more

---

[28] Bradshaw John, *Healing the Shame that Binds You* (Deerfield Beach, FL: Health Communications, Inc., 2005), 21.
[29] Anderson Neil. *The Bondage Breaker* (Eugene, OR: Harvest House Publishers, 2000), 178.
[30] Anderson Neil. *The Bondage Breaker* (Eugene, OR: Harvest House Publishers, 2000), 178.

personal grace becomes, the less personal everything else will feel. Choose the path of grace. It is not easy making grace personal, especially if we struggle with guilt and shame. It has always been difficult for me to accept grace on a personal level, much harder than giving it to others. Those who are more driven or tend to be their own worst critic struggle more with allowing grace to become more personal. Again, this is something that is an intentional choice (more than once), and something that is a journey taking time. The best way to combat guilt and shame on a consistent, long-term basis is to crowd it out with grace. Crowd guilt and shame out of life with grace: the more grace is embraced, the less room there is for guilt and shame to creep in and dominate life. Grace builds us up and enhances our relationship with God and others.

Having identified the problem, made an intentional decision to fight it and embrace the Gospel of Jesus, and made the choice to allow grace to become more personal, we move to the next step of the process of overcoming guilt and shame. If this is the first time you have identified or decided to really confront guilt and shame in your life, you need to determine how deep of an issue it is and how significant of a role guilt and shame are in your life. This cannot be done alone. Begin by talking to those who know you best and get their input. Seek out a professional trained counselor to discuss it.

If it is a deeper issue, engage in regular counseling and read great resources such as *Healing the Shame that Binds You* by John Bradshaw. The more significant a role that guilt and shame have in your life, the more help and work you will need initially. The longer you have embraced the false gospel of guilt and shame, the more work and assistance you will need to overcome that history. Overcoming guilt and shame is not easy work, but it is, in fact, essential work.

Like all things of value, it is hard work, but it is meaningful. It will improve your life, health, faith and relationships. It will lead you on the path to a more meaningful, abundant life characterized by joy and freedom, freedom to be yourself in all situations and circumstances.

Dealing with guilt and shame and overcoming the lies is a journey, one that occurs over a lifetime, one that cannot be taken alone successfully. If you struggle with guilt and shame, whether you had previously realized it or not, you are not alone. I could not begin to count the number of people I know or have encountered over the past decade who struggle with guilt and shame in varying forms and degrees.

I am a diabetic with adult onset type 2 diabetes. I found out I was diabetic shortly after I got married. I went to apply for life insurance like adults do, and I had to get the normal physical and testing. I did not know anything was wrong as I did not feel unwell, or more accurately, I did not realize the way I felt was not normal. The same thing happens with guilt and shame all the time. After I did all my testing, I just waited to get my final premium quote from the insurance company. One day, I got a call stating I was denied for the insurance and needed to call my doctor. Not the kind of phone call you want or expect to get, especially at age 25. I asked some questions and all they could and would say is that they could fax me my lab results.

As I waited for the results, I thought about many possibilities, but fairly quickly my mind went to diabetes. It ran in the family, I was overweight and had a terrible sweet tooth. I consumed Cherry Coke like water. I went online to research diabetes, and quickly realized I had all but one of the symptoms. I knew the problem. I was sad and scared. I was ready though to fight and conquer this disease. I watched my grandmother struggle with it and not take care of herself and as a young, driven, newly-married man, I was not going to let that happen to me.

I called my mother and my new wife and shared the news with them once I got the report. They were both devastated, my wife worrying and my mom blaming herself due to the genetics from her side of the family. To be honest, they were more upset than I was and I had to tell them that maybe instead of talking to me they should just talk to each other, because they were not helping me any at all!

I will be a diabetic for the rest of my life, barring a miracle. There is a high likelihood it will be a part of what ultimately causes me to die. It is something that, if I let it, could rule or ruin my life. It is something that I could, like my grandmother, ignore and allow it to destroy me— and do so far more quickly and painfully than would be necessary. Instead, I chose to fight. I am not a perfect diabetic. I have good and bad seasons. I am told I am better than most, but I refuse to be legalistic, never enjoying certain foods. I also refuse to do whatever I want, because I want to be alive and well to play with my grandchildren someday. It is not going away, but I can manage it, and manage it I do. It is not a one-time effort, but a regular, often daily effort. It is not something I can manage and overcome well on my own. It is a reality of my life, but I do not have to allow it to dictate, ruin or destroy my life. I just have to keep at it. Pay attention to it. Name it. Fight it and refuse to give it power.

The same is true with guilt and shame. They may never go away fully, yet they can be beaten and managed. In order to reject the false gospel of guilt and shame and to continue to overcome its power in your life, you must stay on it, just like I need to stay on top of my diabetes. My health, life, work and family depend upon it. You can deal with guilt and shame if you address it head on and stay on top of it. I can testify that it is worth the hard work. Your health, life, work and family are depending on you to do so, and Jesus walks with you in each moment of battle, in moments of success and failure. You are not alone, and God has something much greater in store for each of us than the toxic lie of the false gospel of guilt and shame.

Important Things to Remember from Chapter 14:

- If the first step is identifying and understanding the problem of guilt and shame, the second step is deciding to seek to both reject and overcome it. It requires an intentional decision. It is not just a one-time intentional decision, but a decision that must be made repeatedly.
- The more personal grace becomes for us, the less personal everything else will feel.
- If this is the first time you have identified or decided to really confront guilt and shame in your life, you need to determine how deep of an issue it is and how significant of a role they are in your life.
- Overcoming guilt and shame is not easy work, but it is, in fact, essential work. Like all things of value, it is hard work, but it is meaningful. It will improve your life, health, faith and relationships. It will lead you on the path to a more meaningful, abundant life characterized by joy and freedom—freedom to be yourself in all situations and circumstances.

CHAPTER 15: GUILT AND SHAME IN THE CHURCH

While the church faces many specific cultural and institutional challenges, the false gospel of guilt and shame is far more dangerous than most, and it is a challenge we have missed completely in the church. Not only has the church missed the challenge of the false gospel of guilt and shame, in some ways the church, intentionally or not, has contributed to spreading it. While the false gospel of guilt and shame is not new, the influence of this lie of the evil one has grown dramatically in the church, especially in North America. The false gospel of guilt and shame is a challenge among every generation and age group in the world today.

The church is called to be a leader in its culture, but far too often we blindly (or not so blindly) embrace the values of the world around us, even if they are contrary to the Gospel of Jesus. The church has bought into the lie that fear should be a motivator and that guilt and shame are not only good teachers, they are values of a Jesus who actually rejected guilt and shame at every turn. The church is a culprit in the rise of guilt and shame in the world and in the lives of people who are created in the image of and loved unconditionally by the God of the universe.

Why has the church embraced the false gospel of guilt and shame, whether intentional or unintentionally? It is a question I have struggled with for years. I have sought answers intellectually, theologically and emotionally. This is an issue that has confused, angered and hurt me, because I see the church as a place where people find truth, healing and love, not lies, pain and rejection. The church, in its attempt to help people, has propagated the false gospel of guilt and shame. The church, in its attempt to address sin and our call to be like Jesus, has communicated in a way that points people to guilt and shame rather than to remorse and repentance, unconditional love and grace. The church in its attempt to take sin seriously and help people change their lives and their behavior has used guilt and shame as a tool to do so. This is wrong, unbiblical, unhealthy, manipulative and not of Jesus, whether intentional or not. The church has failed to do the careful theological reflection of how we communicate truth, both about our sin, mistakes and shortcomings as well as about the unconditional love and grace of God.

I would like to say that the church meant and means well, but that is not always the case. I would like to say that the church did not know better, but whether that is true or not, they *should* know better. It is time for individuals to rise up and reject the false gospel of guilt and shame. It is also time for the church of Jesus to remove any trace of guilt and shame from its teachings and ministries and to stand up against guilt and shame, both in its teaching and in its ministry to the people of the church and their communities who struggle with it. We, as the church of Jesus, have a call, an obligation and a duty to point people to truth, to the no-strings-attached love and grace of Jesus, to offer them the transforming power and abundant life that comes in freely living as God intended us to live.

Guilt is a painful feeling where we focus on our sins, mistakes and shortcomings. If guilt is a feeling about what we have done, shame is an identity. In embracing shame, we embrace the belief that we are nothing more than our sins, mistakes and shortcomings and that those are the things that define us. Guilt and shame are powerful, destructive and often toxic. They have an impact on every area of our life, most profoundly emotionally, spiritually and relationally. Guilt and shame destroy individuals, relationships and communities, and are a cycle that is the driving force behind many addictions and the cycle of addictions. The false gospel of guilt and shame, a lie crafted by the evil one, is a false gospel and a perverted one. It is a direct contradiction to the love and grace at the center of the Gospel of Jesus. Guilt and shame help the evil one to steal, kill and destroy the abundant life for which Jesus died to offer to the whole world.

Guilt and shame do change our hearts, but not in the way God desires and intends, not in a way that brings health and wholeness. Story carries tremendous power in our lives, and we all have the freedom to choose which stories to listen to, believe and embrace. The Gospel of Jesus, the story of the unconditional love and grace of God, is a story of truth. It is a story that brings freedom, joy, health, wholeness and abundant life. It is a story with value and purpose, a story that gives our life value and purpose. The story that is the false gospel of guilt and shame is a lie that seeks to destroy us from the inside out.

If you are battling guilt and shame and have allowed this story to become a part of your story, you are not alone. It is something I have seen many struggle with, people of all ages, beliefs and professions. If guilt and shame have become a force in your life, you are not alone in facing this challenge, and you do not have to be alone in conquering guilt and shame either. Self-knowledge and self-acceptance are two tremendous and important tools in life for finding victory and healing in the midst of guilt and shame. Guilt and shame may be powerful and destructive, but they are a force that can be identified, faced and defeated.

Rather than embrace the lie being sold to us, we must instead embrace the Gospel of Jesus. We must embrace the truth of God's love and grace, the promise that is God's covenant with us. We must not forget some of the most important tenants of our faith: word alone, faith alone, grace alone. Instead of the false gospel, we must embrace the opposite of these ideas found in the true gospel. We must embrace remorse and repentance. We seek to embrace God's unconditional love and grace as we grow in our trust of the Holy Spirit. We have in front of us an incredible opportunity to change the narrative of the church and the world. The harvest is ripe for God to work in mighty ways in the midst of some of the most uncertain and challenging times we have ever faced in the church and the world. The choice is ours.

One thing is for sure: our children do not stand a chance in this world if we pass on to them the false gospel of guilt and shame. We believe in a God who has and who will conquer all. As churches and communities, we are called to be leaders. If we want the life-changing faith found in Jesus, we must fight and reject the toxic mindsets of guilt and shame that have permeated our world and our faith today. The more personal grace becomes for us, the less personal everything else will feel. Choose the path of grace. Which path do you choose in the midst of sin and failure? Which direction do you run when you fail God, those you love or yourself? We do have a choice when we fail, sin or fall short. We can choose the path of truth, love and grace or the path of destruction. Run from guilt and shame and refuse to guilt and shame others. Allow God's love to invade every aspect of your life, and share that same unconditional love and grace with others.

Important Things to Remember from Chapter 15:

- While the church faces many specific cultural and institutional challenges, the false gospel of guilt and shame is far more dangerous than most, and it is a challenge we have missed completely in the church.
- The church is a culprit in the rise of guilt and shame in the world and in the lives of people, people who are created in the image of and loved unconditionally by the God of the universe.
- If guilt and shame have become a force in your life, you are not alone as you face this challenge, and you do not have to be alone in conquering guilt and shame either. Self-knowledge and self-acceptance are two tremendous and important tools in life for finding victory and healing in the midst of guilt and shame.
- The church, in its attempt to address sin and our call to be like Jesus, has communicated in a way that points people to guilt and shame rather than to remorse and repentance, unconditional love and grace.
- Rather than embrace the lie being sold to us, this gospel of guilt and shame, we must instead embrace the Gospel of Jesus. We must embrace the truth of God's love and grace, the promise that is God's covenant with us.

Appendix A:

The Problem of Guilt and Shame

Guilt and shame are two of the most toxic things in our church and culture today. While they are prominent in the culture and church, they are not of God. They are inconsistent with the character and nature of Jesus.

	Truth	Lie
Character	Triune God	Satan
Feeling	Remorse (recognize sin)	Guilt (sin defines you)
Response	Repentance (change)	Shame (self-hatred)
Motivator	Trust	Fear
Emotional Result	Forgiveness (wholeness)	Pain (perpetual)
Disciple	Peter	Judas
Theology	Compelled	Condemned
Biblical Values & Gospel Truth	Love, mercy and grace	None
Spiritual Result	Spirit-filled Life (fruit)	Legalism or Abused Freedom

Which path do you choose in the midst of sin/failure? Which direction do you run when you fail God, those you love or yourself? We do have a choice when we fail, sin or fall short. We can choose the path of truth, love and grace or the path of destruction.

"The more personal grace becomes for us, the less personal everything else will feel. Choose the path of grace."

Bibliography

Anderson, Neil. *The Bondage Breaker.* Eugene, OR: Harvest House Publishers, 2000.

Bradshaw, John. *Healing the Shame that Binds You.* Deerfield Beach, FL: Health Communications, Inc., 2005.

Lewis, C.S. *The Problem of Pain.* New York, NY: HarperCollins, 1996.

Lewis, C.S. *The Screwtape Letters: Includes Screwtape Proposes a Toast.* New York, NY: Scribner, 1996.

Manning, Brennan. *Ruthless Trust: The Ragamuffin's Path to God.* New York, NY: HarperCollins, 2009.

Rohr, Richard. *Things Hidden: Scripture as Spirituality.* Cincinnati, OH: St. Anthony Messenger Press, 2007.

Strong's Exhaustive Concordance: New American Standard Bible. Updated ed. La Habra: *Lockman Foundation, 1995.*
http://www.biblestudytools.com/concordances/strongs-exhaustive-

ABOUT THE AUTHOR

The Rev. Dr. Marcus J. Carlson is an ordained pastor, professor, speaker, writer and consultant. He has almost 20 years of ministry experience in a wide variety of roles inside and outside the church. He earned a Bachelors of Arts in Youth Ministry from Eastern University, a Masters of Theology from Fuller Seminary and a Doctorate of Ministry with a concentration in Youth, Family and Culture from Fuller Theological Seminary. He has additional course work for an MDIV equivalent and Masters courses in counseling. Marcus has served para-church organizations as well as non-denominational, Episcopal, Methodist and Lutheran Churches. He is an ordained pastor with Lutheran Churches in Mission for Christ (LCMC) and the North American Lutheran Church (NALC).

Marcus currently serves as a Lead Pastor in Auburn, IN. Marcus and his wife (and high school sweetheart) Jessica have two children, Micah and Abby. Marcus leads seminars and classes for churches, parents, educators and community organizations. He teaches undergraduate courses in leadership, youth ministry, ministry, theology, ethics and early childhood education. Marcus also teaches graduate courses in ministry, youth ministry, leadership and spiritual formation. You can learn more about Marcus and contact him through his professional website www.revdrorange.com.

Made in the USA
Columbia, SC
15 September 2023